TRAWLING

A group of women gather on Fraserburgh quay to wave off the herring fleet in 1949.

TRAWLING

Celebrating the industry that transformed
Aberdeen and North-East Scotland

Raymond Anderson

BLACK & WHITE PUBLISHING

First published 2007
by Black & White Publishing Ltd,
99 Giles Street, Edinburgh EH6 6BZ

3 5 7 9 10 8 6 4 2   08 09 10
ISBN 13: 978 1 84502 170 2
ISBN 10: 1 84502 170 3

A CIP catalogue record for this book is available from the British Library.

Typeset by
Creative Link

Printed and bound
in Poland
www.polskabook.pl

The photographs drawn from *The Press and Journal* archives can be purchased from The Photosales Department.
Tel: 01224 338011, or by visiting www.weescottishphotos.com

Acknowledgements

My thanks to Tommy Allan, David Craig, John Masson, Rob Kynoch, John Wallace and Donald Anderson for help beyond just allowing themselves to be interrogated; Susan McKay, the staff of Aberdeen Maritime Museum, Professor Callum Roberts and Duncan Smith, Bob Stewart and Tom Cooper of the Aberdeen Journals library.

All the photographs published here came from the files of Aberdeen Journals Ltd, except where noted below.

David Craig, Peter Myers, John Masson and Donald Anderson kindly permitted use of their pictures.

Page xii: A fishing vessel making its way upstream against heavy ice flows 1920s. © Aberdeen Harbour Board/University of Aberdeen.

Pages 77,78 and 79: © Crown Copyright/MOD. Reproduced with the permission of the Controller of Her Majesty's Stationery Office.

Weighing skate at Peterhead in 1968.

To Alix Anderson, the new wave

The fishing boat *Alirmay* of Aberdeen stranded at Downies, Portlethen in September 1949.

Contents

FOREWORDS

It has been a privilege to serve the north-east of Scotland as an elected member of
Parliament for over twenty years. Throughout that time the fishing industry and our proud
patchwork of fishing communities have been the source of the greatest satisfaction, and
sometimes sadness, of my career.

   This fascinating book provides a stark reminder of the danger and demands faced by
fishermen every day, as well as capturing that indomitable community spirit that is the fabric
of our fishing communities and heritage.

   In an inspiring and visually impressive piece, Raymond Anderson wonderfully portrays
the importance of trawling in transforming the north-east of Scotland and I think this work
is a fitting tribute to Scotland's fishermen and their families.

Rt Hon. Alex Salmond, MP, MSP and First Minister of Scotland

Trawling is a well-researched book with great stories of the past, including some that will put a chill down your spine. The book gives an insight into how the fisher-folk lived their lives years ago and I enjoyed reading these yarns that are part of the history of the north-east.

These stories will be enjoyed and spoken about for years to come as we look back at our forefathers' way of life. As a modern day skipper it makes me appreciate the life I have a little more!

Jimmy Buchan, skipper of the *Amity II* of BBC TV's *Trawlermen* series

A steam trawler makes its way through ice in Aberdeen's Victoria Dock in the early 1920s. Note how small the vessels and how open the decks. From the Aberdeen Harbour Board Collection.

INTRODUCTION

INTRODUCTION

Fishing is woven into the very fabric of north-east Scotland. Few families in this corner of Britain do not have links with the sea. Those links run deep in my own family and have given me a particular enthusiasm for tracing the history and development of the trawling industry in text and pictures. I owe a big debt of gratitude to the many photographers who have recorded the multitude of developments and crises that trawling has encountered.

It is little over a century since the industry harnessed the power of steam, sparking growth on an unprecedented scale. Although photography was in its infancy at the very start of steam trawling, the industry was not immediately seen as a subject worthy of recording. No romantic images here for the earliest photographers.

The fishing industry provided hard, dangerous work and everyone connected to it had to show remarkable resilience to survive, let alone prosper. Independence and self-reliance are key elements in the character of north-east folk and that served them well as they established a mighty industry. They also needed vision and skill to embrace technological innovation over the decades as they pursued fish in the hostile environment of the North Sea.

Our fishermen are now among the last of the great hunters left on the planet. Technology has done much to improve the conditions they enjoy but technology cannot remove the hazards of the sea completely.

So will aquaculture one day replace the ships bobbing about on our oceans, risking wave and weather to catch dwindling shoals of fish in what is, by a large margin, the most dangerous industry in the UK? Or is it simply fanciful to imagine that fish farming can begin to meet the market's demands?

And the deep-sea fishers, often with multi-million pound overdrafts to service, cannot even fish freely. Where they cast their nets, how often they fish and how much they catch are dictated yearly by European Union negotiations that are, by their nature, a compromise to placate different countries' political demands.

The writing must be on the wall for the Scottish fishing industry, with all the charts recording a downward trend. Government figures show there were 12,976 regular fishers in 1938 but only 3,813 in 2005. In Aberdeen only 91 regular fishers used the port in 2005,

Peterhead was down to 273 and Fraserburgh rose slightly to 614. The UK had 6,341 fishing vessels in 2005, down from 8,073 in 1996. In Scotland vessels over thirty-three feet declined from 1,144 in 1996 to 718 in 2005.

And yet, after two years researching the north-east fishing industry, I must say I did not find gloom or defeatism. The indomitable spirit of the industry lives on.

Perhaps the hidden ingredient, the X factor of hope, is to be found in the social and cultural roots which endow fishing with a uniqueness born of its hardships, and the unbroken line of generations of families who have plied their trade in the many different branches of what we know simply as 'trawling'. Those family links may not be as strong as they used to be, but they remain an important part of the industry's durability. For the young learner deckhand taking the course at Banff and Buchan College, going to sea is as much a calling today as it has ever been.

Quotas, allowable catches and decommissioning of vessels add an edge to the age-old hazards fishers have faced. But, while they may argue about the severity of cuts and quotas imposed from Brussels and question their fairness, modern skippers do not doubt that conservation of the fish stock is essential if their sons are to have a viable future in trawling. The collapse of fisheries – most famously the Grand Banks off Newfoundland, but also our own herring fishery which declined dramatically in the late 1970s sparking a four-year closure and then a seven-year closure in 1997 – have shown that the oceans are not a limitless provider of food.

Will the words of one opponent of trawling prove prophetic? 'It is clear that the trawlers are carrying destruction to, and impoverishing, the fishing grounds and the spawning grounds of their fish.' That protester, a resident of Torry, was speaking in Aberdeen in 1884.

In the just-published book, *The Unnatural History of the Sea*, Professor Callum Roberts of the University of York sets out a compelling case that bottom trawling cannot continue in its present form. His contention, backed up by a considerable body of research, is that 'intensive trawling is undermining the food webs that support commercial fish species'.

The evidence of collapsed fisheries and destroyed habitats in the world's oceans cannot be ignored.

The seventy per cent of sea that makes our home the Blue Planet is awesome in scale. The longest mountain range on Earth lies under the surface of the sea – the 35,000-mile Mid-Ocean Range. We could drop Mount Everest into the deepest part of our oceans and its summit would be one and a quarter miles beneath the surface. Surely man can devise ways of harvesting the resources of the vast seas without destroying them totally?

The challenge now is to have an industry which is no longer based on ever-increasing catches. With supertrawlers that can now catch 1,000 tonnes of fish in a single haul, major scientific research warns that this could be the last century for wild seafood if current trends continue.

The conclusion of the conservation debate, which started when the first boat dragged its nets across the ocean floor as long ago as the fourteenth century, lies in the future.

This book predominantly concerns itself with trawling's rich past – the events and inventions that shaped the industry, the tragedies that visited fishing communities all too often. Above all, though, it is about the people who helped make trawling such a force in the history of north-east Scotland.

Baskets of fish are swung across to Aberdeen market porters from steam trawlers. The usual time for work to start was 4 a.m.

Having made their point to the nation the fishing boats return to sea at the end of the Aberdeen Harbour blockade in 1975.

1882 The first catch from a steam trawler is landed in Aberdeen, from the converted tug the *Toiler*

1891 Royal Burgh of Torry incorporated into Aberdeen, sparking a boom in population of the former fishers' community

1884 Mass meeting of protest at the new steam trawlers staged in Aberdeen

1889 Aberdeen fish market opened at Albert Basin

1930 270 steam trawlers registered at Aberdeen

1880　1890　1900　1910　1920　1930

1883 First screw-propelled iron trawler built in Aberdeen, the *North Star*, launched at Duthie Yard

1887 Torry's Victoria Bridge completed following ferry tragedy of April 5 1876 in which 32 people perished

1900s Over 4,000 employed in Aberdeen fish industry and curing yards, with a further 2,000 in ship building

1914 Aberdeen largest fishing port in Britain

1925 Aberdeen white fish landings top 2.5 million cwt

Timeline

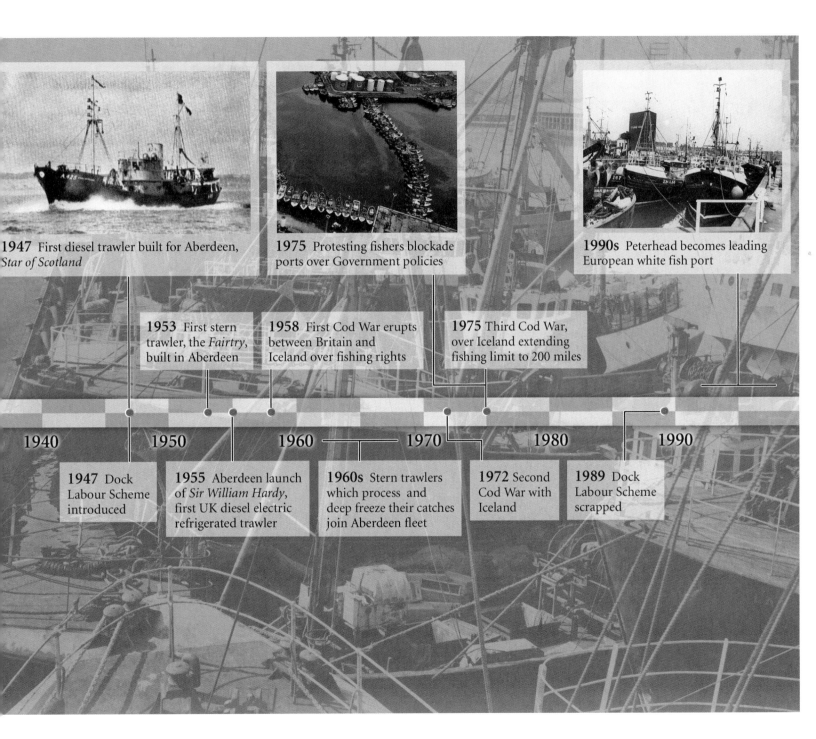

1947 First diesel trawler built for Aberdeen, *Star of Scotland*

1975 Protesting fishers blockade ports over Government policies

1990s Peterhead becomes leading European white fish port

1953 First stern trawler, the *Fairtry*, built in Aberdeen

1958 First Cod War erupts between Britain and Iceland over fishing rights

1975 Third Cod War, over Iceland extending fishing limit to 200 miles

1940   1950   1960   1970   1980   1990

1947 Dock Labour Scheme introduced

1955 Aberdeen launch of *Sir William Hardy*, first UK diesel electric refrigerated trawler

1960s Stern trawlers which process and deep freeze their catches join Aberdeen fleet

1972 Second Cod War with Iceland

1989 Dock Labour Scheme scrapped

Drawing of the Toiler.

TOILERS OF THE SEA

CHAPTER ONE

TOILERS OF THE SEA

On 23 March 1882 a huddle of people gathered at an Aberdeen quayside to see a tiny wooden paddle tugboat set off on a short trip into the bay beyond the harbour entrance. The vessel was appropriately named the *Toiler* and it had been converted to steam power and rigged out for trawl-net fishing. As it set off slowly on its first trip the straggle of people it left behind were largely sceptical of the success of this venture, financed by local businessmen. The *Toiler* did not go far from shore, hauling its nets between Belhelvie and Girdleness. A catch of three boxes of haddock was landed.

This small event, which earned its Aberdeen owners £1 17s (£1.85), marked the start of an industry which was to go on to employ tens of thousands, transform the economy of the north-east and reshape Aberdeen, Peterhead and Fraserburgh. The reverberations of it would be felt in every tiny fishing community along the coast. It was the catalyst for a building boom in Aberdeen that remained unmatched until the discovery of oil in the North Sea in 1969.

The genesis of the trawling industry was not, however, well received by everyone. The line fishermen feared for their livelihoods when the *Toiler* started dragging its nets along the seabed and gave the first hints of the catching power of steam-powered boats.

It was not trawl fishing that the *Aberdeen Journal* was reporting about in that momentous month when the *Toiler* steamed out to the North Sea. The seventh, and last, assassination attempt on Queen Victoria was commanding the column inches. And a great storm raged in northern waters with boats and fishers lost.

Sadly that was not uncommon in those times. The previous year tragedy had visited the fishing families of the north-east with many of the frail line and drift-net boats lost in a mighty gale. The yearly loss in this era was horrendous. In 1848 a bad storm had caught the small, open boats before they had a chance to run for shelter and 124 vessels were lost.

The time had come for change in the fishermen's world.

In 1882 the trade was dominated by sail-powered long-line fishing boats. Great-line fishing took place in deep water for fish such as cod, halibut, ling and skate. It provided a catch of good-quality fish but demanded a lot of work. Each string consisted of a main line with baited branch lines known as snoods.

Small-line fishing was carried out much closer to the home port and was usually operated by families, with women and children responsible for preparing and baiting the hooks with mussel, lugworm or pieces of fish.

Fully mechanised line fishing continues to this day with the prime-condition catches prized by buyers. Great lines can be up to thirteen miles long with, typically, four great lines carrying as many as 12,000 hooks.

But in 1882, just days before the *Toiler* put to sea, the *Aberdeen Journal* reported line-fishing landings of just '4 cwt to 5 cwts of haddock in addition to a few cod and ling'. The catch had been limited by the rough weather with 'fishermen being unable to haul a number of lines which were left in the water'.

Soon it became clear that the twenty-eight ton, fifty-horsepower *Toiler* and its imitators, unfettered by tide or wind, could travel to cast their nets over a greater expanse of sea and catch fish more easily than the established line fishers of the communities of Fittie – as Footdee is known locally – and Torry. The steam power solved the problem of keeping the boat steady while nets were hauled. After a year's operation the value of the fish caught by the *Toiler* had swelled to £3,800, an impressive haul at a time when the total value of fish at Aberdeen market was between £30,000 and £40,000.

It was now apparent that the boat which many fishermen had initially derided was, in fact, dramatically changing fishing. Tensions grew over time as the number of steam trawlers multiplied. In 1883 the first screw-propelled iron trawler built in Aberdeen, the *North Star*, was launched from the shipyard of John Duthie Sons and Company. Members of the *Toiler* syndicate showed their confidence in steam trawling by investing in this venture. The *North Star* was quickly followed off the stocks by two more 'North' trawlers. More than a hundred Duthie-built steam drifters and trawlers were to follow in the next quarter of a century.

But by the end of 1884 matters came to a head in the north-east. Feelings were running high and some of the new boats were even stoned. Added to the concern over lost jobs was the worry that fishing stocks were being seriously reduced. The trawlers also fished on Sundays at this time and the clergy were preaching against the Sabbath being breached. The heady mix of job security, science and religion came to a head in meetings held along the north-east coast from Johnshaven to Nairn. Voices were raised at lively gatherings to petition William Gladstone's Liberal government to stop the 'disastrous and ruinous impact of trawling'.

The most significant mass meeting was held at St Katharine's Hall, Aberdeen, on 10 December 1884, after some 700 protesters marched down Union Street. This great assembly must have been quite a sight as it made its way along Aberdeen's main street, banners flying and a piper leading the way. There was even a fiddler dancing alongside the procession.

The *Aberdeen Journal* reported: 'The movement of such a large body of men excited a considerable amount of interest in the streets. From the squares of Footdee, as well as from Torry, a large number of fisher women were attracted to the scene.'

The meeting itself was conducted in a civilised way with the grievances carefully described. The words of Aberdeen's foremost businessman and political leader of that era, Sir Alexander Anderson, were used to emphasise the importance of fishing to the area. He had told a House of Commons committee that the sea round the shore of Aberdeenshire was a more valuable property for the production of food than the land of the county.

One speaker, from Torry, said: 'It is clear that the trawlers are carrying destruction to, and impoverishing, the fishing grounds and the spawning grounds of their fish.' He pointed out that as the steam trawlers extended the distances they went to fish, the hook-and-line fishermen were left behind.

Interestingly a constant theme at the meeting was the science of the seas – were fish stocks being overfished by the trawlers? Fears were voiced that 'by-and-bye there would not be a fisherman at Footdee Square at all'. Experienced seamen told the meeting of the destruction of fisheries on the south and east coasts of England.

The minister from Slains in Aberdeenshire told of ten fishers leaving the small village of Collieston because trawling had deprived them of their inshore fishings. He added, on a Sabbatarian note, that 'the people were very much grieved to see these trawlers fishing along their shores on the Sabbath day'.

Strong opposition to the views of government scientists rang out in the hall. The scientists' assertion that herring spawned near the surface was derided by the gathered fishers who believed the spawning grounds were on the seabed – and that they were threatened by the dragging trawl nets. (It is now accepted that herring are demersal spawners, depositing their eggs on sand and gravel on the seabed.)

The meeting resolved that 'all necessary steps should be taken immediately by government to prevent the desolation, want and poverty which have come to hook-and-line fishermen of the east coast of Scotland, caused by the present system of steam trawling'. Similar meetings condemning trawling were held by hundreds of fishers at Gourdon and Nairn.

But the mood of William Gladstone's Liberal government was to embrace change rather than stand in its way. And the *Aberdeen Journal's* leader column took issue with the protest meeting. The stone-throwing at trawlers was bracketed with the treatment of Richard Arkwright at the hands of the spinners of Preston when, in 1768, he set to work with his spinning frame. The newspaper pointed out that if more fish are caught it is the public who benefit, and the arguments of spawning grounds being destroyed was dismissed because 'there are only two or three places on the coast of Britain where they are known to spawn'. The fishers were urged to 'lay aside the foolish notion that their interests alone have to be considered'.

Indeed the protesting fishers soon showed the flexibility and initiative of men used to relying on their own resources. One of the stalwarts of the fishing community, Thomas Walker, acted as a spokesman for the line fishermen and confronted Lord Provost Peter Esslemont of Aberdeen about the despised steam trawlers. Mr Walker was advised to 'go and do likewise' – a message he obviously took to heart as he founded the Walker Steam Trawl Fishing Company, which grew to be one of the largest trawler-owning firms in the port.

This was seen as treachery by the men and women of Fittie and Torry and effigies of Tom Walker were burned alongside those of other trawler owners including William Pyper, founder of the North Line and one of Aberdeen's most dynamic businessmen. For once the fishing communities on either side of the Dee were united.

The protests throughout Britain did do some good as they prompted a Royal Commission which came up with some of the first measures for the supervision and control of British sea fisheries.

From 1878 there were remarkably detailed investigations reporting to parliament on all aspects of commercial fishing. In 1883 the Fishery Board for Scotland even offered advice on how long it should take to gut, cure and pack catches. But on steam trawlers they were adamant that 'the wealth of the sea is so enormous that no improved appliance for adding to the food of the population ought to be discouraged'.

In 1884 the *Aberdeen Journal* published a letter from a Macduff reader saying 'the public at large are getting cheap fish and fish that they never got before. I consider the trawlers benefactors to the public'. The days of stoning trawlers passed, setting the scene for a remarkable period of growth in Aberdeen. Within a decade of the *Toiler* putting to sea Aberdeen was the largest whitefish port in Scotland.

The need for an improved fish market was becoming clear and a deputation of business leaders was dispatched south to see how other ports were coping. On the advice of these men a market was built at Albert Dock. One of the deputation, William Pyper, later wrote:

Before the fish market, wives and daughters of the fishermen had to toil up the braes from the shore with their loads of fish, take their creels to Aberdeen and sit for hours in a dirty and unhealthy fish market, returning home in the afternoon with bundles of provisions.

The new market was even seen as a special attraction with 'thousands of visitors going to South Market Street in the course of a year to gaze upon the interesting sight of the fleet of fishing vessels discharging their catches'.

With trawlers staying longer at sea it became necessary to find some way of keeping the fish fresh and ice was imported from Norway. There was an initial hitch when the customs officials could not find a relevant duty category for this cargo. The load was impounded until a decision was reached on how to classify the ice. After much deliberation it was agreed that the cargo should be designated as 'dry goods'. But, sadly, by the time this was agreed the 'dry goods' had turned to water. By 1890 Aberdeen had its own ice plant thanks to a consortium of trawler owners.

Aberdeen landings from trawlers grew inexorably from 55,260 cwt (2,763 tons) in 1888 to 378,200 cwt (18,910 tons) in 1935. The tonnage landed reached one of its peaks at 2,355,000 cwt (117,750 tons) just before the outbreak of World War I. At that time 218 trawlers fished out of Aberdeen.

Many people were needed to service the trawler landings at Aberdeen – 2,763 landings in 1888 had grown to 18,910 in 1935. The core trades of catching, curing and marketing were only the tip of the industry. As well as the workers of the fish houses, there were ice makers and ship chandlers, net makers, ship repairers, engineering shops, coopers and fish meal manufacturers. They were all part of an essential army of ancillary workers serving the fleet.

In addition, of course, the transport operation grew along with bigger landings. Trains and lorries had to be available to take the fish nationwide as quickly and efficiently as possible. The Aberdeen railway station, being so close to the docks, was a real benefit. And the shipbuilding yards flourished on a high tide of activity that demanded more and more trawlers.

Bustling Aberdeen drew people from the fishing villages of north-east Scotland, and much further afield, including the colourful trawlermen from English ports such as Scarborough, Grimsby and Yarmouth. With their high-heeled boots, drainpipe trousers, flowing jackets and brass earrings they cut a piratical appearance which was rather shattered by the popularity of bowler hats among these men. According to a writer of the time they were 'much addicted to wine and women', although he granted that this was 'no doubt as an antidote to the rigours of their calling'.

All these migrant workers had to be housed. Torry was ripe for growth after the Victoria Bridge, spanning the River Dee, was opened officially by Queen Victoria in 1887. The bridge was the city's response to the ferry disaster of 1876 in which thirty-two people died. The tragic sinking of an overloaded boat caused the separate Royal Burgh of Torry to be linked to the city, and eventually incorporated into Aberdeen in 1891.

Within a year of the fish market at Albert Basin being opened in 1889 it had to be extended as the steam trawler fleet grew. Girls in long oilskins and boots became a familiar sight. Wearing shawls pinned over the shoulders of their woollen jerseys and with tightly tied headscarves they could be seen walking in groups from Torry to their work at the harbour fish houses. Like the migratory workers of the herring fisheries they protected fingers from sharp knives and piercing fish bones with 'cloots' – rags wrapped around their fingers.

From 1881 to 1891 the Torry population boomed by almost 2,000 to 2,993 and from 1891 to 1901 some 9,386 went to live in the new tenements built to cope with the dramatic change that a converted tugboat had brought to the city. The scale of the growth of steam trawling and its impact on Aberdeen at the dawn of the twentieth century outstripped the oil boom that the same city was to see some seventy years later.

Torry grew rapidly into a small town to service the new industry. In 1881 the population of Aberdeen topped 100,000. With the help of the fishing boom the number of citizens doubled in the second half of the nineteenth century. In 1905 the *Aberdeen Journal* calculated that the fishing industry provided work for 9,200 people and 2,600 of them were preparing and curing whitefish.

By 1914 Aberdeen was the largest fishing port in Britain. In 1924 whitefish landings in the port topped 2,500,000 cwt (125,000 tons) for the first time. The following year even higher landings were recorded, but these levels were never to be reached again. At that time it was reckoned that up to 40,000 people in Aberdeen – one quarter of the population – earned money from the fish trade. By 1930 the port was home to 270 registered steam trawlers.

Ethel Kilgour, in her memoir of being brought up in St Clements in the 1930s (A *Time of Our Lives*), paints an evocative picture of the harbour in those busy days:

South Market Street was a great hub of activity. Great Clydesdale horses pulled drays of fish boxes and coal, the unloading of which from the coal boats seemed to go on unceasingly, raising clouds of dust. It was a busy, noisy scene with the smell of fish strong in the air.

The interwar years saw increasing competition from German, Dutch and Norwegian boats. Aberdeen's distance from the main population centres of Britain also put pressure on profits as landings slowly declined.

In 1946, helped by the fallow years of World War II, the trawl nets bulged with fish again and landings soared.

The fishers' ability to adapt came to the forefront in the postwar years. Diesel engines arrived in 1947 when the *Star of Scotland* became the first motor trawler built for Aberdeen owners. By the 1950s the true worth of this new breed of trawler was clear to see as the fleet shed its ageing steam trawlers. In 1957 the *Star of Scotland* showed what diesel could achieve with a record-breaking 133-hour return trip to the Faroe Islands. Skipper Andrew Baxter ran the trawler 740 miles and made fifteen fish hauls.

The more powerful diesel engines were just one of a succession of technical and safety measures which over the years greatly improved the fishermen's lot. Powered block winches helped to haul the nets, decent lighting illuminated the boats and new designs provided more cover and protection for those on the deck.

The first full-scale factory stern trawler, the *Fairtry*, was built in Aberdeen in 1953. It incorporated freezers and pointed the way ahead for the fleet.

In 1955 another milestone was reached with the launch of the Sir William Hardy at Hall Russell's Pocra Quay slipway. She became the first UK diesel-electric refrigerated trawler thus revolutionising the preparation and storage of catches. Her experimental work for the Ministry of Agriculture, Fisheries and Food's Torry Research Station set a new standard for trawler fleets. Diesel-electric power, in which a diesel engine is connected to an electric generator, brought many benefits. There was increased control of ships with greater manoeuvrability, better fuel efficiency and less maintenance.

The *Sir William Hardy* had a productive twenty-three-year career with MAFF and then became famous again when bought by the environmental campaigners Greenpeace and renamed the *Rainbow Warrior*. Surely the only Aberdeen trawler to be blown up by the French secret service, she was controversially sunk in Auckland, New Zealand.

The *Rainbow Warrior* has near legendary status in the world of environmental campaigning. The ship was involved in direct action against French nuclear weapon testing in the Pacific in 1985. While anchored in Auckland the *Rainbow Warrior* was sunk by explosives and one man died. In the ensuing international furore the French minister of defence resigned, two agents were jailed and massive compensation was paid to New Zealand and the Greenpeace organisation by the French government.

Through the 1960s and 1970s the Aberdeen fleet remained at over a hundred vessels, but the trend was one of declining landings, although the industry continued to innovate when stern trawlers which could process and deep-freeze catches at sea were introduced to the north-east fleets.

The decline was hardly surprising as the industry was hit by one body blow after another. Quayside prices fell, costs rose, access to fishing grounds became restricted and catch quotas were imposed. In April 1975 fishermen blockaded ports around the coast of Britain in an outpouring of frustration by men who felt abandoned and betrayed by the government.

Aberdeen fishers had the added complication of the burgeoning oil industry and its demands for harbour space. By 1980 the fleet in Aberdeen scarcely deserved that title with only twenty-five trawlers remaining.

In the House of Commons on 3 May 1989, Scottish Secretary Ian Lang highlighted another of the factors in the fleet's decline. Speaking in defence of the scrapping of the Dock Labour Scheme he said: 'Between 1977 and 1987 business through Aberdeen fell by twenty per cent. Over the same period the number of fish landings at Peterhead rose by eighty-four per cent.'

And while the end of the Dock Labour Scheme – introduced in 1947 to give workers protection from unscrupulous employers but latterly blamed for restrictive practices – gave Aberdeen Harbour the flexibility to compete better with the neighbouring ports, the shift of fish landings to Peterhead from Aberdeen was consolidated.

Further signs of the decline of Aberdeen as a fishing port came in August 2007 when the Commercial Quay fish market was demolished. With insufficient landings to justify a planned £3.5 million upgrade by the Harbour Board, the underused facility was razed, leaving the city with only the Palmerston Quay market. A far cry from the days when 300 trawlers jostled for space at Aberdeen's quaysides.

While the first century of trawling was spent devising ever more powerful trawlers and ever more sophisticated ways of detecting and catching fish, the future is likely to be different. A leaner and fitter industry has shown remarkable dexterity in adapting to the era of the Brussels bureaucrats. The demands to conserve fish stocks will surely only increase. Whatever the future holds for trawling it is certain that it has made an indelible mark on north-east Scotland.

Striking trawlermen are held behind a barricade at Aberdeen Fish Market in August 1969 during a ten-week strike over wages

Getting down to work at Aberdeen's new fish market in April 1982.

Fishermen angry at their treatment by the Government staged spectacular protests throughout Britain. This is the protest at Aberdeen Harbour where they used their boats to blockade the entrance in 1975.

The fishing boat blockade at
Peterhead Harbour in 1975.

The trawlers head
back to the fishing
grounds after the
protest ended.

Work gets underway to demolish the Palmerston Quay section of Aberdeen Fish Market in February 1974, at the start of another upgrading of the port's facilities.

August 1974 and work on creating a new fish market is underway at Palmerston Quay, South Market Street, Aberdeen.

Looking south over Aberdeen Fish Market and the harbour's Albert Basin in 1986.

An impressive halibut catch
at Aberdeen in 1960.

Two market porters chat as trawlers
are unloaded at the fish market that
was later replaced. This was in 1964
and wicker baskets and wooden boxes
are still in use.

Victoria Bridge, Aberdeen.

THE SKIPPERS

CHAPTER TWO

THE SKIPPERS

As David Craig and Tommy Allan slipped into the relaxed banter of old friends it was easy to underestimate the depth of knowledge and experience in the trawling industry these men embodied.

The pair were chatting in David Craig's office overlooking Aberdeen harbour's Albert Quay. As the only two skippers in the port still surviving from the days when trawlers navigated by sextants (which measure the altitude of the sun or a star in order to determine a ship's position), talk inevitably turned to the sea.

Trawling is still regarded as one of the most hazardous of occupations, but in the 1930s there were many more perils. David, who had not long turned ninety, at the time of this interview said: 'There were no generators so there was no electricity. The captain had to navigate by dead reckoning. He only had his sextant to help him.'

Tommy is troubled with 'seamen's legs' but, apart from that painful legacy of long hours standing on trawler bridges bracing against the roll of the boat, he remains remarkably spry and enjoys making regular trips into Aberdeen from his Ellon home to see former colleagues.

Quick to recall people and places from the past, he has a natural modesty. Although I know him to have been a first-rate skipper he would only admit to doing 'nae bad', adding that he was 'always in a job'.

With a mischievous smile David pointed out that Tommy is older than him – by all of thirty days.

Many of Tommy's years at sea were spent working for George Craig and Sons, the firm founded by David's father in 1933.

Unlike the majority of trawler firms that failed to adapt to a changing world, the Craigs embraced the challenges of the North Sea oil bonanza with spectacular success. A Texan oilman turned up at the firm's harbour office in the 1970s with a request for a trawler to work as a safety vessel for a North Sea oil rig and sparked a chain of events that took the company into a new world.

By 2006 David Craig was chairman of a company with a near £100 million turnover and bases spread across the globe. The Craig Group has interests from oilfield services and fishing to marine electronics and catering. It also has a leisure division. And despite being a quarter of a century past the normal retirement age when I met him, David was active in his role with a particular responsibility for the firm's fishing boats.

All those momentous changes were a lifetime away when David and Tommy first met at Torry Primary School. David went on to Robert Gordon's College but the pull of the sea was too much and he joined Aberdeen's trawler fleet aged fifteen.

It was in 1932 I started to sea as an apprentice. There was no training prior to that. You went aboard as a 'deckhand learner'. When you could box the compass and do a few other jobs you became a 'sleeping deckhand' – as you didn't haul the nets you got more sleep. You did that for about a year. You were like a cleaner.

In those days there was no electricity on boats. We had carbide lamps. We put calcium carbide in tubes and added water to produce gas for light. But you weren't allowed to use that for navigation, you had to use paraffin oil lamps for that.

Tommy, who went to sea at eighteen after four years as a filleter in the fish trade, recalled the introduction of electricity to ships as a huge leap forward. 'The first time I went aboard a boat with electric lights I was delighted. No more dashing about the deck in all weathers hauling oil lamps up the mast.'

The rewards for the deckies trying to keep the lights going and hauling them forty feet up a mast on a vessel bucketing about on the sea were not generous.

'When I started going to sea my pay was 7/6d (37.5p) a day as a deckhand,' said David. 'And you had to pay for your own food out of that.' But at least the crew were assured of a wage; the skipper and mate got paid a share of the catch. A poor trip could be disastrous for them. David recalled that when he was a mate he had to borrow from his mother to pay for his food.

One early advance which David appreciated was an echo meter to record the depth of the sea.

We started getting an echo meter on board and that was a great help. It was fantastic. It saved us taking a lead. When you were a sleeping deckhand the skipper would call out 'dip the lead' and then when you got the soundings and knew the depth of the sea you had to pull the whole long line back. I had great muscles with that.

George Craig senior recognised that his son David was ambitious and gave him every opportunity to advance his sea career. David said:

In 1936 I had my Mate's Ticket and then you had to go in the capacity of a mate for one year before you could take your Skipper's Ticket and you couldn't be a skipper until you were twenty-one. I was twenty-one in April and took the ticket in June so all those things worked well for me as my father had ships and I was a mate right away. I was one of the youngest skippers in Aberdeen. In those days there were 280 boats fishing from Aberdeen.

A heavy responsibility lay on those young shoulders as the new skipper headed out to sea on his first command, the trawler *River Ness*.

Then, as now, the skipper was at the heart of the industry. He was the man who had to hunt down the fish to keep everyone else in a job. In the 1930s the bridge must have seemed a lonely place for the skipper. There was precious little to help him in his job. As David recalled:

In those days there was no wireless communication. Without generators there was no electricity. There was nothing. So when we went away to sea you were on your own. A captain was on his own, he went by his own dead reckoning and his charts. The only other aid a captain had was his sextant.

The skipper has absolute control on the sea. The owners leave them to use their judgement on where to fish. Tommy pointed out the flip side of that freedom: 'If you don't get it right you get the sack.'

It is the skipper who has to choose when to shoot the gear; a vital decision which only he can take. If his experience is trusty he will know where to go at which time of year to get good catches.

Individual skippers had their favoured areas. Tommy said: 'Some bits of the fishing grounds you'd keep to yourself.' The skipper's 'little black book' would also be scrutinised. 'Every skipper has a book of where to go and when,' explained Tommy. 'A diary of fishing successes and failures.' But in those pre-European Union days the seas were open to the skippers. 'We could go anywhere and weren't hindered by regulations,' said Tommy.

As the trip progressed the pressure increased on the skipper. If the cod end wasn't filled with fish, there were the worries of paying the fuel and bank bills. There was also the responsibility for up to a dozen men on a trip of up to eighteen days. Their wages had to be covered by the catch.

Even a good trip was not without its strains. A routine developed of shooting the gear, towing for three hours, gutting the fish before you hauled the nets again. Eventually only a few hours of sleep would be snatched as work continued through the night.

And crewmen couldn't look forward to too long at home at the end of a trip. After being away for eighteen days if the trawler had to sail to the further flung waters of Iceland and the Faroe Islands, fishers would be back at sea with only two days spent ashore. Tommy said: 'Sometimes you would make your landing on a Tuesday morning with the boat's catch landed the next day and you would only have one clear day at home before you were away to sea again.' Like all fishermen Tommy missed out on most of the special family occasions. Many birthdays and weddings were celebrated while he was at sea.

Then there was the added complication of the weather which Tommy freely admitted could be very scary.

He ruefully recalled his days lying off Aberdeen in storms waiting to run the 'bar'. This is the point where the salt seawater meets the freshwater of a river, a clearly defined line between two distinct colours on fine days but in a swell it becomes a particularly rough stretch of water that pitches boats around. Aberdeen's 'bar' is notorious among seamen for its ferocity.

On rough days there were lines of cars on the Nigg Road with people waiting to see boats coming in, and I was on the bridge shaking. One minute you were heading for the Beach Ballroom, the next you'd be going towards Cove.

For Tommy and David's generation there were more than storms to contend with. Both men had boats sunk under them during World War II.

Fate caught up with David off Shetland in June 1940. He was skippering the *River Ness*, towing nets, when a lone Nazi Dornier aircraft attacked them, dropping three bombs. The crew rushed to cut the nets free so that the boat would be more manoeuvrable while David sent out a Mayday call. Just as he had finished this the plane returned and there was an explosion as the ship was hit. For a time his leg was trapped as water rushed into the vessel. At last he released himself and rose to the surface as the *River Ness* slipped below, dragging David down with it for some terrifying moments until he got to the surface dazed and slightly injured. His mate, James Christie, swam to him. The pair were trying to rejoin other crew members on a liferaft when the Dornier returned and strafed the area and the crew. Only David and the mate survived the attack.

In November of 1940 Tommy was serving on a new ship, HMS *Chestnut*, minesweeping in the English Channel, when it was blown up. All the crew survived with only slight injuries.

During the war years only a limited and carefully controlled amount of fishing took place.

David recalled with the delight of a born fisherman the big catches in 1945 after the war ended. He was fishing in seas which had not seen a trawler in five years. For six months his holds were bulging with fish as he virtually had the seas to himself. Other trawlers were discouraged by the continuing danger from German mines in the seas. He was in command of the *Copieux*, a newly purchased trawler badly in need of refitting.

'When the first six months was over I went to my solicitor and he said, "David, you can stop fishing whenever you like and get repairs done. You've paid for your boat now."'

David gained the nickname of the Turbot King through his ability to catch that highly valued fish in those postwar years of plentiful catches.

Despite all the political and conservation pressure on the fleet with limited catches, decommissioning and ever-increasing costs, David remains optimistic for the future. Drawing on the experience of a lifetime chasing the shoals he said: 'The North Sea is one of the most prolific fishing areas I've known in my life. There's a mixture of fish everywhere you go.' But the challenges are considerable: David considered the problems of 2006.

This is the worst year that the fishing industry has experienced since we joined the Common Market. There's only a third of the fishing fleet left. For example, five years ago there were about 400 to 500 boats fishing out of Peterhead. They're down to about 160 whitefish boats now.

And just as in 1882 when the trawling industry began in Aberdeen there is debate between scientist and fisher about the best way to preserve fish stocks.

David Craig fears that decommissioning the fleet is not doing the job it intended. 'You would think that over a space of years you would see an increase in the amount of fish, especially cod, but you're not. Scientists are now coming to believe what the fisherman has been shouting about – global warming.' Much still remains to be learned about the movements of the shoals and the effects of warmer water on the fish and their natural food stocks.

'But I'm confident for the future if we get a chance . . . fifty days at sea, that's all we're allowed in 2006. Now, how can you run any industry like that? If Brussels cuts the quota again we're finished.'

Tommy Allan (left) and David Craig at Albert Quay, Aberdeen. Both of the former skippers were ninety years old when this picture was taken in 2006.

Aberdeen Fish Market with sales still in progress at 11.30 a.m. in April 1965. A breakdown in negotiations between the porters and the vessel owners on overtime payments for Saturday landings sparked a ban. This action by the porters had trawl owners calling in their boats before the weekend and the market was swamped with landings. There had to be double sales and the market floor was not closed until well after noon. The action caused merchants to stage a Saturday auction in private premises. Fish were consigned from Buckie, Stonehaven and Arbroath but the sale was a flop with only 150 boxes.

Fish market porters at work unloading the Aberdeen trawler *Scottish King* in 1969.

Fish are unloaded from a trawler at Aberdeen in 1974.

A good catch of fish on show in 1975 at Aberdeen's new market.

An unusual sight for Aberdeen Fish Market in 1983. This is a midnight discharge of a catch. For many years the starting time at the port had been 4 a.m. but the *Clarkwood*, under the command of skipper Stuart Thomson, docked with a very heavy catch – 2,000 cwt – and an early start was agreed to get the catch turned out in time for sale at 7.30 a.m.

Shouting out the prices in 1977
at Aberdeen Fish Market.

The *Grampian Crest* being built for the George Craig Group in 1959 at Hessle on Humberside.

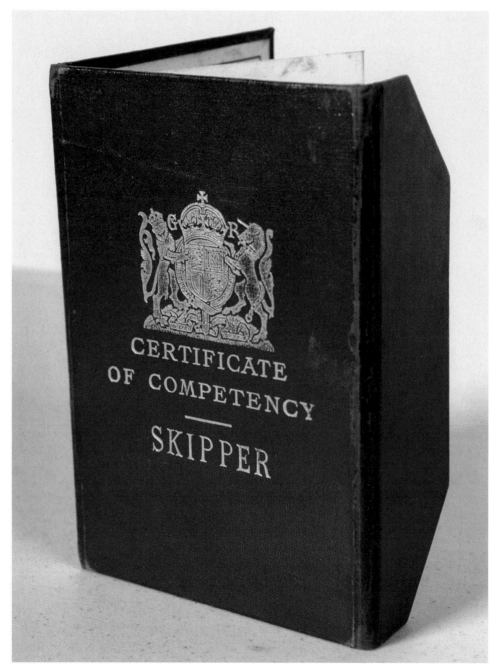

The coveted Skipper's Ticket, the certificate which permitted its owner to be master of a trawler. This certificate, dating from 1925, belonged to Andrew Baxter, skipper of the first diesel powered trawler to fish out of Aberdeen.

STRANGE

PEOPLE

CHAPTER THREE

STRANGE PEOPLE

The popular view of the character of the north-east of Scotland fishing families was eloquently stated by John R. Allan. 'Strange people; they are mostly radical in politics and very conservative in their way of life. They are good people.' The writer, farmer and broadcaster was commenting in the County of Aberdeen section of the *Third Statistical Account of Scotland* published in 1960. Even then, however, John Allan recognised that the exclusive nature of the north-east fishing communities was undergoing inevitable social change.

But in 1882 when the *Toiler* first trawled the waters off Aberdeen the seafront community of Fittie would certainly have seemed a place apart to other Aberdonians. Known as Footdee to the town council and map-makers, those in the community only ever refer to it as Fittie. They consider Footdee to be a ponderous affectation. In their tidy squares, which the council provided in 1809, the people huddled together in a society shaped by the dangers faced by the men who worked the uncertain North Sea for a living.

For, like those in the villages that dot the north-east coast, Fittie folk were servants of the sea, living in tiny societies which had evolved to a remarkable extent for the sole purpose of sustaining the fishers.

One nineteenth-century writer noted of Fittie: 'None live within the square but the fishermen and their families so that they are completely isolated and secluded from public gaze as a regiment of soldiers within the dead walls of a barrack.'

Traditionally the man of the household supplied the fish which was sold at market by the older women with the young, stronger women carrying the fish to the selling place. The women had arduous lives. Before the advent of steam trawlers they not only looked after the fish sales but also baited lines and shelled mussels early in the morning before seeing to the children and running the household. All this, of course, with the men usually away. Little wonder that these remarkable women got a reputation of having their men tied to their petticoats. Or, as John Allan put it: 'Men that could face the stormiest seas with maybe a psalm tune for comfort, sang sma' when they got inside their own doors.'

And crucially it was the women who kept hold of their household's money. All these communities recognised the truth of the old saying that 'no man can be a fisherman and lack

a wife'. Here I have to declare a bias as my mother was born in a fisher's cottage in the North Square of Fittie. When I started noticing how things were in the early 1950s the family had all moved away from Fittie.

By then my grandfather, Andrew Baxter, was a skipper, as was his son, also Andrew. The demands of a large family and the relatively good rewards of the trade had seen a move to Aberdeen's West End. But Fittie still loomed large for our family. Unquestioningly recognised as the source of sound values, this was often expressed succinctly by grandmother Jane Baxter as 'cleanliness is next to Godliness'.

This was a long-established maxim. A writer in the 1860s said of Fittie that 'the interior of the houses is as clean, sweet and wholesome as could well be desired . . . a picture of tidiness such as is seldom met with among classes of the population reckoned higher in the social scale'.

And the Godliness was also taken seriously by my grandmother. The church was a large part of her life. Along with her husband she sang in the choir of St Clement's Church. Even as a child I understood that when the family sang Hymn 626 they were not just mouthing words of no significance. When the voices rose towards the chorus 'O hear us when we cry to Thee for those in peril on the sea', the full import of these words was not lost on anyone in the family.

Fittie was, however, not always considered a haven of Christianity. At one time swearing to tell the truth on the bible in the courtroom was taken so casually by the fishing fraternity that a new oath was devised for them. It ended with the memorable words: 'If I do not speak the truth may my boat be a bonnet to me.'

The unruliness of the earlier Fittie community, clustered close to what is now the Victoria Dock, is probably exaggerated but there certainly was lawlessness, sometimes connected to protecting the community's perceived fishing rights from strangers. And which community so close to the sea didn't indulge in a little smuggling in those far-off days?

There were two great waves of religious revival that had a profound effect on the fishing communities. The first came in 1859 and 1860. A Captain Summers of Fraserburgh is credited with converting many in Fittie. He sailed to Aberdeen from Leith, where the revival had taken hold, and conducted meetings which filled halls to the rafters.

The long-term effect of this conversion can be judged by the attitude in Fittie towards alcohol. Drink – and drugs in the modern era – are certain temptation to men who daily endure the rigours of the North Sea. But Fittie remains a dry area to this day. In 1860 there were three public houses. All eventually closed.

Fittie also produced its share of missionaries who carried the word around the world as far as China.

The 1921 revivalism was linked to a year of storms and tragedies at sea. A year when the vital herring landings were poor. The religious fervour which swept the land seems to have started in East Anglia with open-air preachers who gathered ever larger crowds. One of the most famous of those preachers was a cooper from Wick, Jack Troup.

As the word spread up the coast it was said it was not uncommon to see women so affected by the preaching that they wept as they worked among the fish barrels at Peterhead and other north-east ports. Perhaps the north-east rallies of the evangelist Billy Graham in the 1960s are the closest we have seen to this in more recent decades.

Literally thousands turned to religion for solace. One man, Peterhead cooper James Turner, was credited with converting 8,000 in two years. And it was not just the mainstream religions that people embraced. Different Brethren movements attracted a following along the north-east coast.

'Fishermen are as a rule serious minded folk, living perpetually in an atmosphere of anxiety,' wrote Hugh Mackenzie in the *Third Statistical Account of Scotland*. 'They have the ever present fear of losing a son, a husband or a brother at sea . . . making them turn to religion for comfort and solace more than most people do.'

For my grandparents a strong faith was a bulwark against the blows of an uncertain life as surely as the thick seaward walls of Fittie's North Square was a bulwark against the waves.

World War II did much to sweep away the old order. It seems that even the superstitions of fishermen altered with the social change that a World War ushered in. Where once a fisher would be afraid to put to sea if he saw a minister on his way to the boat, now it is the washing machine that cannot be used on the morning of a trip to sea, all that churning water suggesting a storm. Instead of having to make sure the coast was clear of men of the cloth, the wife now has to put up with the inconvenience of a delayed wash.

Sometimes there seem to be as many superstitions as there are seamen. In the old days you would never begin fishing on a Friday and today a crewman may consider that clearing out the sugar bowl at home is essential to a successful trip. But even in our enlightened times you may find a fisher who will never utter the word 'rabbit' on a trawler or will only refer to salmon as 'red fish'.

At one time it was unusual to find a seaman who could swim. It was said that if the worst befell them it was better not to prolong the agony. For the same reason the big leather seaboots that were once part of every trawlerman's gear would take them right to the sea bed if they ever went overboard.

Today my family's last physical links with Fittie have died out. One of my first journalistic assignments took me to Fittie to interview an artist living there and I was surprised to be recognised by relatives. But that was forty years ago and I would go unnoticed now. The area has become gentrified and the old fisher's cottages are sought after in an age that values authenticity and links with the past.

The squares are a conservation area with prices of over £100,000 for the but-and-bens in 2006. An interesting premium on the prices paid when they were bought from the council around 1880. Then they fetched from £85 to a top price of £180. This once-unique and vibrant community is now described in property registers as 'a quaint and historic former fishing village'.

The days when there were so many Baxters and Allans, Guyans and Caies, Fowlers and Nobles in Fittie that they had to have by-names are gone. Colourful distinguishing names like Bowfer, Pokie's Dod and Tootsie's Minnie were given to ease identification, a practice followed in all the north-east fishertowns.

While it would have been difficult to identify a specific Baxter among so many, I wonder if the by-names did not sometimes get a little out of hand. One person was known as Rachles'-Jock's-Lizzie's-Jim. With Rachles being the by-name of the man's great-grandfather this was more a family history than a name. Such convoluted titles were by no means uncommon in the fishing towns. Perhaps it is understandable that Fittie folk were once considered by outsiders to have their own dialect.

When my grandfather was a young man – and sons followed their fathers to sea – marrying a girl from outside his community would have been frowned on. Indeed up to World War II it was considered unacceptable for a young man to take a bride from a neighbouring village, let alone a distant town or country. My grandfather told me that for a man or woman from Fittie to marry someone from across the River Dee in Torry was not the done thing. That alone shows just how much has changed in little more than fifty years.

Fish boxes are filled from creels at Aberdeen in 1964.

One of Aberdeen's last fishwives pauses for a brief cup of tea at her stance in The Green in 1948. Bundles of hard dried fish are spread around her for sale.

During a break at Peterhead Harbour in the 1930s the work still continues for the fisher lassies. They are knitting for their menfolk.

A fishwife with a creel on her back in 1938.

Fishwives with creels on their backs at Peterhead Harbour in 1935. In the background a horse-drawn trailer can be seen loaded with coal for the port's steam trawlers.

The *River Ness* crew take a break for a mug of tea and a photograph in front of the bridge in the 1930s.

The George Craig and Sons trawler *River Ness A110*.

Trawlers at Pointlaw in the 1960s.

Superintendent Neil McGregor in the Memorial Room at the Fishermen's Mission in Fraserburgh.

THE MEMORIAL

CHAPTER FOUR

THE MEMORIAL

There's one room in Fraserburgh where the sacrifice of the north-east fishing community can be keenly felt. Anyone visiting the Fishermen's Memorial Room will appreciate the price that is paid all too often to put food on our tables. The room, in the Royal National Mission for Deep Sea Fishermen, is lined with brass plaques in tribute to seamen who lost their lives. They are aged from just sixteen years to seventy-two years. Although the memorial covers only the towns and villages in the short coastline from St Combs to Banff, there are 116 names on the walls.

The importance of this remembrance room can best be judged by the visitors' book with its expressions of love and loss. That sense of loss is deepened in sea tragedies when the loved one is never found. The Mission is only too aware of the hurt felt if there is no grave to mark a death, with no headstone to visit or lay wreaths against.

Like the quiet and confidential work which the Mission and its officers provide to the community, this room meets a deeply felt need. Superintendent Neil McGregor of the Fraserburgh Mission said: 'The Memorial Room highlights the need of fishermen's families to have a place to come to, simply to remember. And throughout the year that is what happens.'

On the walls of the memorial room are the brief details of the great tragedies of this area – the loss of three lifeboats within living memory.

The plaques detail the lifeboat *Lady Rothes*, lost with two crewmen in 1919, and the *John and Charles Kennedy*, which turned turtle at the harbour entrance in 1953 as it escorted a fishing vessel to safety. Six men drowned. One crewman survived.

Those losses must have been in the minds of Fraserburgh folk when in 1970, in the harsh month of January, they started to gather at the Fishermen's Mission on the harbour front. Word was spreading of fears for the lifeboat *Duchess of Kent*. Could it really have happened again? A third lifeboat lost?

But the worst fears were confirmed. *The Duchess of Kent* was overwhelmed in huge seas as she went to the rescue of a small Danish shrimp boat. Remarkably John Jackson Buchan, who had been on lookout on the deck, was plucked to safety by a Russian ship. He arrived back at Buckie with the bodies of four of his comrades (while a fifth was lost at sea). Five

women had been widowed and fifteen children left fatherless.

Thousands turned out to mark the passing of the five seamen. Coxswain Johnny Stephen, Fred Kirkness, James Buchan, James Slessor Buchan and Willie Hadden had been volunteers who unquestioningly braved storms to help others. In the church there were only four coffins in front of the mourners. The body of Fred Kirkness had not been recovered. A space was left beside the coffins of his colleagues. Survivor John Jackson Buchan died in 1999, aged 76.

Despite the tragedies that visited Fraserburgh's lifeboats there was never any real question of the town not having a lifeboat to safeguard those who fish around that exposed knuckle of land that punches out into the North Sea.

A new lifeboat, the *Willie and May Gall*, arrived in May 2002 continuing a tradition that stretches back to 1858 when the RNLI opened a Fraserburgh station – the first in Scotland.

The end of a poignant mission for the Buckie lifeboat crew as they bring to shore the sole survivor of the Fraserburgh lifeboat tragedy. The bodies of his crewmates lie on the boat deck as John Jackson Buchan steps off the lifeboat.

Thousands are packed into the Kirkton cemetery but still the mourners arrive to pay their last respects to the Fraserburgh lifeboat crewmen who died on the *Duchess of Kent*.

The Duke of Kent leads mourners as they walk down Fraserburgh's Broad Street behind the cortege of crewmen who died when the lifeboat *Duchess of Kent* was overwhelmed in a storm.

An attempt by coastguards to get a line aboard the *Ben Gulvain* grounded at Balgownie in 1976.

The trawler *Ben Gulvain* leaves Aberdeen Harbour for the fishing grounds in happier times. This picture was taken in 1967.

A crewman is winched to safety by a helicopter from the Aberdeen trawler *Ben Gulvain* grounded at Balgownie in 1976.

Waves cascade over Aberdeen Harbour's south breakwater as a trawler heads for its berth on a stormy day.

THOSE IN

PERIL

CHAPTER FIVE

THOSE IN PERIL

Fishermen and the rescue services of the seas have been inextricably linked down the generations. Inevitably it was from the ranks of fishermen that most lifeboatmen came. From the beginning of the nineteenth century open lifeboats, based at Fittie in Aberdeen, were launched into the surf to carry out rescues. Hundreds owed their lives to these proud, brave men.

So it was hardly surprising that the RNLI's new motor-powered vessel was not universally welcomed by traditionalists when she arrived at Aberdeen in 1923 on a round-Britain demonstration tour.

However, fate took a hand in this lively debate when the trawler *Imperial Prince* ran aground off the Black Dog north of Aberdeen just weeks after the motor lifeboat visited the port. It took five hours to get a boat alongside the trawler. Two men perished and seven were rescued but a major row broke out over the quality of equipment available to the rescuers.

It was clear that the heroic launching of a lifeboat on a carriage into the pounding surf by brute force had no future. Within two years Aberdeen had its own RNLI state-of-the-art motor lifeboat berthed at Pocra jetty.

Among the many stories of bravery connected to the *Imperial Prince* rescue was the one of the young reporter who stripped off and attempted unsuccessfully to swim out to the stricken vessel through the gale-whipped sea with a lifeline. George Ley Smith was a Scottish water polo international who went on to become editor of the *Press and Journal*.

The motor lifeboat *Emma Constance* had a long and distinguished service. In September 1927 she was called out when the trawler *Ben Torc* ran aground at Greg Ness Point in fog. The lifeboat manoeuvred alongside the trawler and her five crew managed to leap aboard the bucking boat. But skipper George Rose, noted for wearing a bowler at sea, plunged into the sea. When he surfaced and was eventually hauled to safety aboard the lifeboat he was still wearing his bowler.

On Christmas Day 1935 the *Emma Constance* took part in a rescue that did not have such a happy outcome. Darkness had descended and a high sea was running when the Aberdeen trawler *George Stroud* made the run into the harbour across the broken water of the 'bar'. As she entered the navigational channel a wave struck her and flung the vessel against the

North Pier sending her crunching and grinding along the wall before coming to rest 200 yards from the harbour entrance. The five men aboard, who minutes before had been looking forward to seeing their families again for the Christmas celebrations, were suddenly in dire danger.

The *Emma Constance* was at the scene within minutes and making efforts to get alongside the trawler as most of the crew sheltered in the wheelhouse. Lifeboat coxswain Tom Sinclair saw a pinpoint of red light in the darkness on one of his approaches to the boat. The light came from a cigarette held by cook Sandy Wood who was grabbed by the lapels as the two vessels came together and hauled to safety.

By this time a crowd had gathered on the pier with onlookers weeping openly as they watched the tragedy unfold. A rocket line was fired to the trawler but soon the wave-battered wheelhouse started to break up. Only one crewman managed to secure himself to the breeches buoy gear to be hauled ashore. Three men died. The battered lifeboat, with only one engine in operation, continued to search the storm-tossed waters for survivors for an hour after the last trawlerman was saved.

On 4 November 1937, the *Emma Constance* was being refitted, so it was reserve lifeboat *J & W* that was the number one vessel on duty. She had already been called out once that day – to the grounded *Delila*, which was helped free from a sandbank near Belhelvie – when Newburgh folk raised the alarm. They had heard siren blasts but could see nothing in the poor visibility.

Only when a lifebelt washed ashore was it known that the Aberdeen trawler *Roslin* was in distress. It was 2 a.m. before the lifeboat crew saw the Roslin aground and almost submerged by the pounding waves. Four of the crew had sought refuge in the rigging and the other four sheltered in the wheelhouse.

The weakest of the men in the rigging lost his grip and fell to the deck. After a half-hour struggle in the foaming waves near the mouth of the River Ythan a line was thrown to the three men still clinging to the rigging. It took six attempts before a survivor finally managed to grab the line. That seaman then tried to secure the most distressed of his crewmates to the rope but the man slipped from his grasp before this could be done and was swallowed by the sea.

The remaining crewmen outside the wheelhouse fastened themselves to the line and leaped into the sea to be dragged to safety. The men in the rigging had heard their crewmates singing hymns as they sheltered in the battered wheelhouse. Tragically a wave lifted off the roof and swept the men to their deaths. Six men died.

The rescue operation lasted seven hours. The RNLI awarded Coxswain Tom Sinclair its silver medal for gallantry and bronze medals went to Second Coxswain George Flett and acting mechanic Bert Esson.

It was the second time that year Tom Sinclair had gained a silver medal. When he retired in 1949 he had been twenty-five years with the RNLI and had saved 200 lives. Tom, who also gained a bronze medal for gallantry, had a near legendary reputation for his steely calm in dangerous situations.

It was on 31 January 1953 that a great storm battered sea and land causing the worst natural disaster in northern Europe for 200 years. A rapid-moving low-pressure system swept across the North Sea whipping up very high winds – one sustained wind at Costa Head, Orkney, was recorded at 125 m.p.h. This wind combined with a high tide which overwhelmed flood defences. Over 150,000 acres were flooded and 307 lives lost in the UK but in the Netherlands over 1,800 people drowned and vast swathes of land were left under water. Seamen who were at sea in that storm will never forget its ferocity or that eleven vessels were lost off the British coast.

In November 1959 another storm raged across the north-east bringing chaos on land and sending ships running for any shelter they could find. But one lifeboat headed out to face the full fury of the seas. The lifeboat was from the small Banffshire village of Whitehills and the events of that terrifying rescue trip were to be recalled for generations as the night of the three miracles.

The lifeboatmen were going to the assistance of a Dutch coaster with broken steering gear and the eleven people aboard drifting helplessly towards Scotland's rocky coast in the storm.

As the tiny vessel and its eight-man crew began the rescue mission in the storm-lashed Moray Firth a huge wave tossed the lifeboat's bows high into the air, throwing one crewman into the sea and flipping over the boat. William Lovie, the former coxswain of the lifeboat and a man who had spent his life at sea, said later: 'I have never seen a wave like the one that hit us. It was like a mountain.'

Then fate took a hand.

Miracle Number One was when another massive wave thundered against the lifeboat's bows and righted it again. Coxswain William Pirie explained later: 'Our lifeboat is not a self-righting boat and when she turned over we all thought we'd had it.'

Miracle Number Two came after crewman Alexander Johnstone, who was standing outside the shelter of the cockpit, was thrown overboard. Incredibly he saw the burning light of the overturned lifeboat as he struggled below the surface of the ink-black water. When the vessel righted itself Alexander found he was just an arm's-length from the boat. He grabbed a rope and was hauled aboard. Afterwards he said:

> If the lifeboat's engines had not stopped when she overturned I would have been lost. They would have gone on, the crew would not have heard me shout for help and they would not have seen me on a night like that. But the engines did stop.

Miracle Number Three was in the form of a light glimpsed through driving rain and clouds of seaspray. After turning turtle the Whitehills lifeboat engine restarted but the compass light had been smashed and the radio was out of action. While those on shore feared the lifeboat lost, the crew endured the storm. For three and a half hours they rode the waves expecting at any time to be capsized again.

Then the faint blink of Covesea Lighthouse, on tiny islands three miles west of Lossiemouth, was identified and the men set course for Burghead. But even when they eventually reached that harbour their ordeal was not over. The storm made it impossible to enter the haven and they had to shelter as best they could until daylight, when they set course for the shelter of Cromarty where their fourteen-hour trial by sea ended. After they made land Coxswain Pirie looked over the now glittering and calm sea and said: 'That's the way it usually is after a storm. No wonder they call it the cruel sea.'

As the Whitehills lifeboat battled for survival, another drama was unfolding at the coaster *Geziena Henderika* as the crew took it in turns to guide the crippled vessel with emergency steering gear.

When the coaster had sent out an SOS the Whitehills and Burghead lifeboats had gone to her assistance, joined by the Aberdeen trawler *Dunkinty* and an oil tanker. When the situation on the coaster seemed hopeless the call was made to abandon ship. But the mate's wife was a passenger and when she refused to leave the ship the crew decided to remain with her and wait for the worst to happen.

Late at night as the storm raged, the *Dunkinty* manoeuvred alongside the stricken Dutch coaster. Twice the trawler's crew threw a line to the coaster. Both broke under the tremendous strains caused by the waves. But a third line held and the two ships, now lashed together, made for land. After a thirty-hour drama they finally made the safety of Inverness. A sea epic had ended against all the odds without loss of life.

The changing face of sea rescue was clear for all to see in January 1976 when the trawler *Ben Gulvain* became stranded 200 yards off the Royal Aberdeen golf course at Bridge of Don.

A breeches buoy rescue was attempted but failed. The crew was then winched to safety on one of the Sikorsky helicopters which had become an increasingly common sight in the skies above Aberdeen as the offshore oil operations gathered pace.

Whether it is frail boats pushed by hand into the waves from the beach or rescue from the skies, the bravery and commitment of the rescuers remains constant to this day.

While it is an undoubted fact that trawling has become safer, it remains the most dangerous industry in the UK by a factor of five. The North Sea will always have the ability to inflict tragedy.

There was a cruel reminder as I compiled this book. Within weeks of my learning there were long-serving men at the Aberdeen lifeboat station who cannot recall the last time they were called out to help a trawler in distress, the *Meridian* went missing. This trawler was from the small fishing community of Anstruther. A prawn and herring fishing vessel, it was working as a guard boat for an oil pipeline when a signal was picked up from its distress beacon. The crew of four who were lost in that October 2006 force 10 gale came from Fife and Aberdeen. Only one body was recovered.

An open lifeboat is hauled through the surf by a line of men during the *Imperial Prince* rescue drama at Blackdog, near Aberdeen, in 1923. Two crew perished on the grounded trawler and the old-style carriage-launch lifeboats were heavily criticised.

Lifeboat *John and Robert C. Mercer* going to the grounded Aberdeen trawler *Delila* in November 1937, the same day that the *Roslin* foundered. The *Delila* was helped free of a sandbank. That day lifesaving craft were launched from Belhelvie, Newburgh, Collieston and Bridge of Don as well as Aberdeen.

The lifeboat *John and Robert C. Mercer* approaches the trawler *Delila*, near Belhelvie.

The dramatic wreck of the *Ben Screel* at Girdleness in January 1933 after the vessel missed the entrance to Aberdeen Harbour in thick fog.

The seas are calm as the crippled coaster *Geziena Henderika* arrives at Inverness lashed to the Aberdeen trawler *Dunkinty*, (left). This peaceful scene from November 1959 is in stark contrast to the previous thirty hours in which the Whitehills lifeboat turned turtle, a lifeboatman was swept into the sea and the *Dunkinty* fought through storm-whipped seas to get a line to the crippled coaster. Miraculously no lives were lost in the drama. As Coxswain William Pirie of the lifeboat remarked about the calm that followed his crew's ordeal: 'That's the way it usually is after a storm. No wonder they call it the cruel sea.' (Story in Chapter 5)

An Aberdeen trawler approaching the harbour in the huge seas of the Great Storm in 1953.

A trawler is struck by a large wave during a storm at sea in 1972

Crossing Aberdeen's rough 'bar' in the late 1950s. The ship taking the buffeting is the *George Craig*.

COD WARS

CHAPTER SIX

COD WARS

During the first Cod War an Aberdeen trawler dramatically clashed with a Faroese gunboat, sparking headlines across Scotland. The incident was all the more newsworthy because two schoolboys were aboard the fishing boat. I was one of them.

However all was not quite as it seemed in this July 1960 drama. Yes, there had been an incident. But it did not involve the vessel I was on, the *Star of Loretto*. My uncle, Andrew Baxter, had relayed the distress call from the trawler involved, the *James Robb*, and the true story had become confused. It was nonetheless an interesting introduction to one of the perils of fishing in the late 1950s and early 1960s – and a cautionary tale about the accuracy of news reports.

I was on the trawler because my uncle was keen that generations-long family links with the Aberdeen fishing fleet continue. He had three daughters and as the son of his eldest sister I was the obvious choice to continue this unbroken inheritance of the sea. My young companion on the trip, Ian Grimmer, was keen on a seagoing career and was also experiencing his first trip. He was the son of the trawler's second fisherman, Fred Grimmer.

Although we were well looked after there is no easy introduction to life on a trawler. Aberdeen Harbour's choppy 'bar' quickly brought home to the young guests the reality of a relatively small vessel ploughing up and over the broken water where seawater meets freshwater. Our sea sickness made us feel wretched. Being reassured that many an experienced seaman suffered as badly every time they went to sea was little consolation. I did recover from this and got my 'sea legs' as the days passed.

Then came the news that a Faroese gunboat was tangling with a Scottish trawler and a Royal Navy corvette had been called to the scene. The first of the Cod Wars started in 1958 when Iceland sought to protect its rich fishing banks and the industries they supported by extending the island's coastal limits from four to twelve miles. That started years of friction as Iceland and the Faroe Islands attempted to enforce their arbitrary rulings by arresting and fining offending trawlers.

Britain argued that international law supported only three-mile limits and the trawlers continued to operate in the fishing grounds they had used for generations. Capture within banned grounds could be an expensive business for trawlers, with heavy fines imposed and confiscation of catch and fishing gear.

Over the years of the Cod Wars half a dozen Icelandic coastguard patrol boats were deployed, most famously the *Thor, Aegir* and *Odin* which had skirmishes with Royal Navy frigates. But they were ill-matched against the swift naval vessels. The trawler *Northern Foam* was arrested within the twelve-mile limit during the first Cod War then retaken by the Navy. Crew members of the *Thor* were taken from the trawler to the frigate *Eastbourne*, leading to a mob of protesting Icelanders stoning the British Ambassador's home in Reykjavik. It was a most unseemly way for fellow members of the NATO alliance to behave, but the harrying tactics and occasional rammings were set to continue for years.

The first Cod War ended in 1961 when Britain acknowledged the twelve-mile coastal limit and was permitted to fish up to a six-mile fishing limit. An awkward 'ceasefire' continued until 1972 when Iceland extended its territorial waters to fifty miles.

This 'war' was shorter but more dangerous than the first. The Icelanders had developed a secret weapon – a net cutter. Coastguard vessels would cruise astern of trawlers dragging a wire cutter which severed the wires of the trawl gear. This adaptation of minesweeping technology parted sixty-nine trawlers from nets and catches. There were high-speed rammings and eventually an Icelandic gunboat blew a hole in the hull of a trawler. The navy moved into the area and trawlers had to fish in 'boxes' so that the frigates could do their policing job. This was all disastrous for the catches and an interim agreement in 1973 allowed British trawlers a limited annual catch with further restrictions on fishing areas and numbers of trawlers.

But trouble flared again in 1975 when Iceland provoked the third Cod War by imposing 200-mile territorial waters which provoked fury in Britain and brought relations between the two countries to a new low.

Iceland threatened to close its NATO base. This was viewed with alarm by the military authorities in those days of that other, far more serious, confrontation – the Cold War with Russia. NATO stepped into the dispute.

This was the shortest and sharpest of the national confrontations. For seven months there were rammings and trawl-gear cutting. Shots were fired again. More than fifty trawlers had lost their trawls to the net cutters when Foreign Secretary James Callaghan tried to calm matters, saying that while 'both sides in the conflict are showing valour, there is no need for anyone to show their virility'.

After fresh negotiations the 200-mile ban remained and British trawlers were allowed an

annual catch of 50,000 tons with restrictions on the numbers of vessels permitted within the limit. While the dramas at sea were grabbing the headlines the effects on shore were drastic throughout Britain, with 1,500 fishing jobs reckoned to have been lost and 7,500 onshore jobs also going.

My own trip during the Cod War ended at Aberdeen fish market where the local reporter waiting at the quayside learned he was pursuing a red herring and the headlines of youngsters being menaced by Faroese shells were inaccurate.

After that eventful trip my family found I didn't speak about going to sea again.

I had seen the fishers on deck gutting all night with their hands red raw and bleeding. My enthusiasm for a life at sea had gone.

The Royal Navy frigate *Mermaid* (right) and the Icelandic gunboat *Baldur* come perilously close to each other during high sea jousting in the Cod War of 1975. (RAF Kinloss)

A pond of fish ready to be gutted and iced at sea.

The Naval frigate *Mermaid* (top) moves to thwart the gunboat Baldur as she protects the British fishing fleet during one of the Icelandic Cod Wars.

Royal Navy frigates chase Iceland's *Aegir* as she moves behind a British trawler in an attempt to cut its trawling gear. This picture was taken within Iceland's disputed fifty-mile territorial waters in 1973.

High seas and blizzards. The sort of conditions endured in Icelandic waters during the Cod Wars. This scene was captured in 1975 on a supply vessel servicing Royal Navy vessels protecting the British trawl fleet from Iceland's gunboats.

Sign of a healthy port, the bustling quayside at Peterhead in 1986 when more berthing space was a priority.

PORT OF

VISION

CHAPTER SEVEN

PORT OF VISION

The port of Peterhead has had the benefit of three great waves of prosperity. Whaling, herring and whitefish each in turn brought boom to the most easterly town in Scotland.

It is not hard to see why Peterhead's natural shelter has been a welcome haven to sailors for 1,000 years. In the tenth century Viking longships sought the refuge of the inlets protected by two islands, later named Greenhill and Keith Inch. After all, the knuckle of land which contained this shelter was their first westerly landfall after leaving the Scandinavian coast, a welcome sight for any Norse warrior who had sailed 400 miles of open sea.

By the mid-sixteenth century Peterhead's natural harbour had developed into a port with berths and jetties. And before the century was out a bulwark and primitive breakwater had helped provide greater shelter from the North Sea. By the eighteenth century Peterhead was a popular port, with channels widened, piers constructed and the island of Keith Inch joined to the mainland. North and South harbours sheltered vessels from the Baltic, England, Hudson Bay and Greenland. Work on the port's distinctive long sweep of breakwaters began in 1886 and continued through to 1956.

Whaling ships first set out from Peterhead on their hazardous journeys in 1788. By 1840 it was the top whaling port in Britain and by 1857 the harbour was home to thirty-two whaling ships. This grim, hard trade continued through to the 1880s. From 1820 the loss of men and ships became very high when large catches lured boats to the dense, packed ice of the Davis Strait between Greenland and Baffin Island.

Peterhead lost eight of its ships in that deadly strait from 1826 to 1832. The privations of the crews were terrible; trapped in ice for a winter, they would have to survive as best they could on meagre rations of salted meat with the ever-present risk of scurvy. If ice breached the vessel the crew would have to try to survive the cold on deck or worse. In 1830 the whaling nations lost nineteen vessels in the Davis Strait and at one time 1,000 men were camped on the ice awaiting rescue. Little wonder that returning seamen also told of cases of insanity. At least twenty-four Peterhead ships were wrecked in the hunt for whales.

Indiscriminate slaughter of any creature can only last so long and whaling went into a long decline, finally dying out in 1893, after just over a hundred years. By then the next boom – herring – had grown to the point where it was dominating the port's business.

In the summer herring fishery the population of Peterhead swelled by up to 5,000. By 1896 there was enough work for seventy-four fish-curing companies. At the outbreak of World War I the Scots drifter fleet approached 1,000 boats, but after the war major markets such as inflation-hit Germany and post-Revolution Russia had disappeared. The long years of contraction had begun for the herring fishers.

In the 1960s catches plummeted as overfishing continued. Later the greater catching power of the purse-net fishing method took its toll. With purse-seining large shoals of mid-water fish are surrounded by a huge curtain-type net which is then closed around the fish by mechanised power blocks. A large purse-seine net is over half a mile long and 650 feet deep. A catch of 400 tons of herring can be taken in one shooting of the net. In 1977 an east coast ban on herring fishing had to be introduced. It stretched to four years and was followed by strictly regulated fishing.

The most easterly haven for boats in the British Isles has been well served by providence. But the bounty of the seas has not always been fully understood. Excessive whaling killed off that trade and the herring shoals were fished to the brink of extinction.

Hopefully lessons have been learned and the whitefish, which have brought so much prosperity to the port, will not go the same way as the whales and herring. The awesome catching power of today's supertrawlers certainly make conservation absolutely vital.

In his book *The Port of Peterhead*, A. R. Buchan speculated about Peterhead's future. He wrote: 'Now [1977] undreamed of quantities of fish are landed at Peterhead. £30-million worth in a single year will be achieved in the next year or two.' The 'undreamed of quantities of fish' at Peterhead exceeded £100 million in 2006, albeit that pelagic fish, that shoal near the surface or in mid-water, made up half of this total. Much higher prices are also a big factor in the value of catches.

So how did Peterhead surpass Aberdeen to become the top Scots port and go on to become the main whitefish port in Europe? Peterhead had the advantage of being a private port which was not part of the National Dock Labour Scheme. The tradition of skipper-owners certainly handed the port an advantage during the industrial relations turbulence of the 1960s and 1970s. Donald M. Anderson, a Peterhead skipper for thirty-six years, who fished out of Aberdeen for two winters, put his problems with the fish-market staff starkly: 'Every time I landed in Aberdeen I had trouble wi' the lumpers.'

By the time the Dock Labour Scheme was finally scrapped as an anachronism in 1989 many had voted with their feet and Peterhead had taken over Aberdeen's mantle as the top

Scots port. The Dock Labour Scheme was seen by the unions as a necessary protection against the indignities of the casual labour system. Others, however, saw it as a jobs-for-life system which gave the unions a stranglehold on the docks.

The Peterhead system that proved so attractive to the merchants of the twentieth century had a long history. Even the Peterhead whaling crews of the eighteenth century signed up to a system of shares of the catch and fishing crews traditionally shared in a boat's profits.

When boats got bigger and more expensive, loans from the curers to a small proportion of the Peterhead fleet inhibited the bargaining strength of some fishers on the market floor. However, even this tie was slackened by the crash of prices in the 1880s. Catches became too large for the market and prices were so low that profits disappeared and bankruptcies followed.

Fishers were badly hit and had to become more efficient to survive, cutting crew sizes and reducing the size of the fleet. During this shake-out the boat-engaging system came to be replaced by an auction system for the fish.

The port of Peterhead also has much to offer in the way of facilities, particularly since the very successful merger that took place between the Peterhead Bay Authority and Peterhead Harbour Trustees to form the Peterhead Port Authority on 1 January 2006.

The new port has a strong record of reinvestment and supports fuel supplies, ice and water plants and ship repair and maintenance facilities at a slipway, shiplift and dry dock, in addition to the UK's most modern chilled fish market.

Prosperity continues to flow from the port's third wave of opportunity. In the five years up to 2002 £35 million was invested in the harbour and there are plans for a £20 million redevelopment of the Smith Embankment scheduled to begin in the spring of 2008 to provide further all-weather deep-draught berths.

Mackerel and herring continue to be an important part of Peterhead's pelagic trade now that stocks are judged to be healthier. These return half of the fish-related income. Five major companies have since based their operations at Peterhead, making it the number one port in the UK for both pelagic and demersal species – the upper-water and deep-water fish.

Of course, it is just possible that many at Aberdeen harbour were not entirely sorry to see the shift of fish markets to Peterhead, given that it happened during the North Sea oil boom and Europe's oil capital had a new demanding and cash-rich industry to service. But Peterhead, once again benefiting from its easterly position, is also a key base for the offshore oil industry.

Famous engineers such as Sir John Goode, John Rennie, John Smeaton, Robert and David

Stevenson and Thomas Telford all made their contribution to the Peterhead harbour development from the eighteenth century. Today the bustling, diversified port of Peterhead is a testament to their skill and the foresight and energy of successive port trustees and administrators. John Wallace, current chief executive of the Port Authority commented:

Peterhead has clearly a varied and proud seafaring history and it is upon this foundation that the town and port have prospered. Given this gritty determined past, it is no surprise that the new Port Authority is so well equipped and placed to meet the challenges in the fishing and oil industries for many years to come.

Stormbound trawlers crowd the berths at Seagate, Peterhead Harbour, in 1981.

Expert eyes are cast over a huge consignment of whitefish at Peterhead in 1969.

Brisk business as salesmen work their way through the fish sheds at Peterhead Fish Market in 1980.

Veteran seaman Donald M. Anderson.

Fish are tipped from the traditional wooden boxes into new plastic containers at Peterhead in 1987.

Crew gut fish on the open deck of the *Rononia* in 1950.

PRESERVATION AND INNOVATION

CHAPTER EIGHT

PRESERVATION AND INNOVATION

The never-ceasing work to preserve fishing stocks was continuing aboard the *Solstice II* as she lay at berth in Fraserburgh's Balaclava Harbour, swept by cold winds and rain on a day in early autumn. The 62-foot trawler was having a refinement added to its nets to help conserve fish stocks in the North Sea for future generations.

The work was being overseen by Rob Kynoch of the Fisheries Research Services (FRS) in Aberdeen, who had worked on the net designs to release young fish quickly. Rob was letting me see at first hand the technological revolution which had swept the industry since I had last been on a trawler forty-five years previously when radar was the prized technological innovation.

Today the bridge of a Scottish trawler contains an array of electronic equipment. The skipper dials in a setting which then plots the way to his destination. The computerised plotters not only take the trawler to the fishing grounds but also give all the information of previous trips – the modern equivalent of the skippers' black books that contained notes on all their fishing experience.

There are sounding devices and sonar and radar equipment, engine monitors and monitors for the nets. CCTV cameras give the skipper a view of those areas of the ship once invisible from the bridge.

Small joysticks, seeming more appropriate to a computer-game console than a trawler's bridge, manoeuvre the vessel and there is a duplicate control desk at the rear of the bridge for when the nets are shot – all controlled by the skipper.

Rob pointed out other advances in the design of boats. The deck, once open to the elements, is now covered in. Trawlermen, who I vividly recall gutting on a deck swept by rain and wave, now have a station within the vessel where the fish and prawns are delivered down a chute to a conveyor belt at which they are prepared for the market, boxed and iced.

Many of these advances and improvements to the trawler fleet started in north-east Scotland. The FRS helped develop the conveyor belt used on trawlers. Rob is full of admiration for the skippers of today.

I don't think people appreciate how knowledgeable they are. These guys have to really understand electronics. There's so much sophisticated equipment now, like the global positioning systems and sonar. There are computers for controlling the temperature in the hold and equipment for shooting the nets.

Looking around the Balaclava Harbour at Fraserburgh that grey day, it was possible to see it as a microcosm of the industry. The trawlers like the *Solstice II* were clustered together preparing for sea, while moored close by were pelagic supertrawlers. These 200-foot vessels are packed with the latest electronics and have catching power the fishers of old could not comprehend. There are eighteen based in the north-east and, as Rob pointed out, they can net as much as the 5,000 herring boats which used to be based in the area. But quotas and limited allowable fishing days at sea mean these multi-million pound investments spend most of their time tethered to the dock.

However, after twenty years of working with the trawl industry from the marine laboratory, Rob remains confident that it has a good future despite yearly problems with Brussels and the Common Fisheries Policy. The fishing-gear expert told me he detected the tentative beginnings of a renaissance for the industry, particularly in Aberdeen. Rob said, 'It's heartening at the moment, there's a lot of optimism out there.' Although Aberdeen has no fishing fleet as such, he sees it as an increasingly popular port of call for the migratory fishing fleets from Britain and Europe.

In his time he has seen many changes as technology has played an increasingly important role. 'The skippers are very open to new technology and their fishing practices have changed,' said Rob.

The FRS is a government agency that provides expert scientific and technical advice on marine and freshwater fisheries, so Rob is pleased to note that skippers now 'know they must let young fish away to spawn'. He adds:

> The new skippers are not going for the bulk 'lifts' of fish. At one time skippers were judged by the weight of the 'lifts' from the sea – up to 16–17 tons. But these included many fish which were not marketable. Now it's all quality they're after. The bulk mentality has gone and we have a different breed of skipper.

These days we need to look at independent trawl fishers as medium-sized to large firms with an investment in that business which often runs into millions of pounds. Rob would, however, like to see more young people on the boats: 'You find that the youngest crewmen are in their mid-to-late thirties.'

The trawler *Craiglynne*'s helmsman Jim Murray keeps an eye on the compass as he sets course for Aberdeen in 1973. Picture by Peter Myers.

The *Craiglynne*'s net is hauled in as trawling continues through the night in this picture from the 1970s. Picture by Peter Myers.

The cod end is swung aboard the Aberdeen trawler *Craiglynne* during a trip in 1979. Picture by Peter Myers.

Trawlermen gutting the catch on the open deck of a trawler in April 1972.

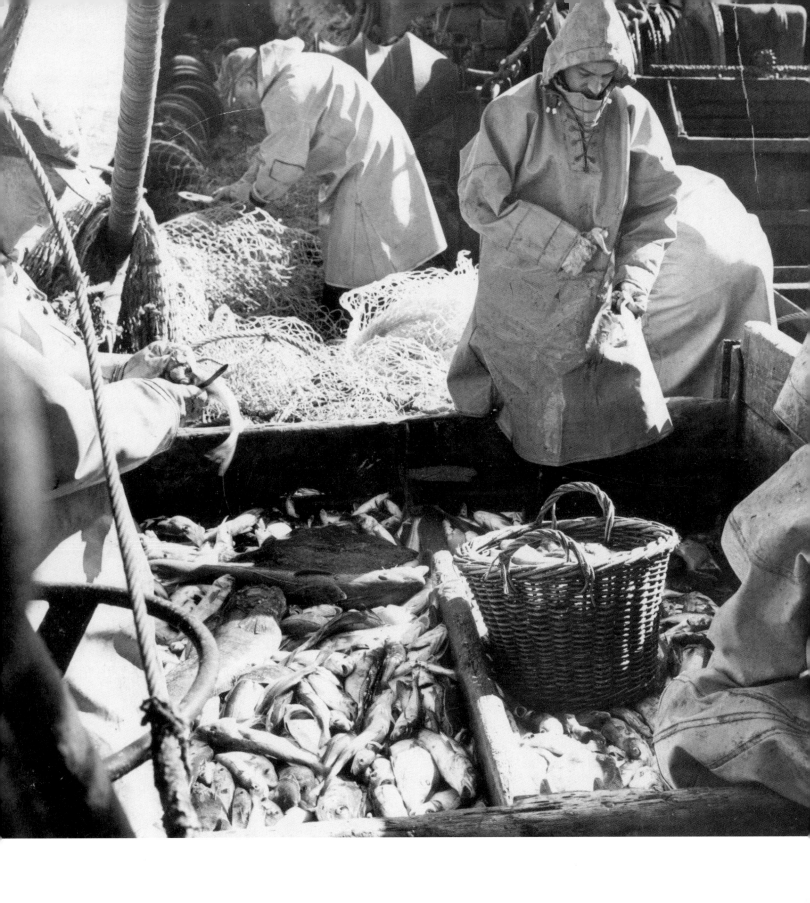

Some trawlermen gut the latest catch while others repair nets in preparation for the next 'shoot'.

David Craig, left, gutting fish on deck with crewmates.

A bulging cod end is swung over the deck.

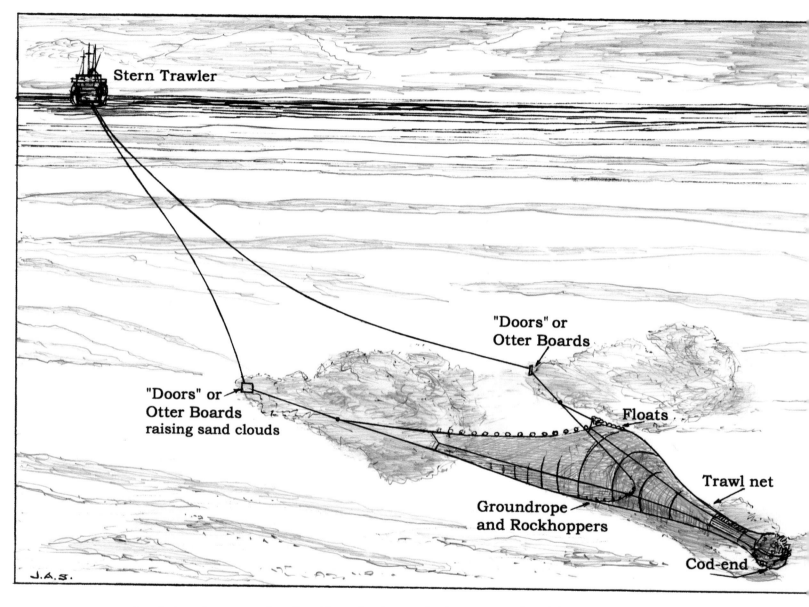

Stern Trawler

"Doors" or
Otter Boards

"Doors" or
Otter Boards
raising sand clouds

Floats

Groundrope
and Rockhoppers

Trawl net

Cod-end

J.A.S.

A typical trawl net set-up for a Scottish trawler showing the doors, or otter boards holding the net open, the floats giving height to the net as it is towed along the bottom with the nets protected from stones and debris by rubber rockhopper discs. The doors are traditionally made of wood reinforced by steel. Today deep-sea fishers favour steel doors specifically designed for ease of use.

CASTING THE NETS

CHAPTER NINE

CASTING THE NETS

The nets which the *Toiler* used to fish the North Sea more than 120 years ago would still be recognisable to a trawlerman in today's hi-tech industry. The *Toiler's* nets had a beam, a strong bar which holds the net open, and a frame at each end, all this towed by the trawler. Rob Kynoch of FRS in Aberdeen said:

> The height of the frame, what we call 'shoes' at either side of the net, dictated how far the net top was from the seabed, but they were very low to the seabed then. That was the initial stage before they introduced trawl 'doors' in 1894 which is basically what we have now. At first fishers just set the 'doors' – timbers strapped together and protected by steel plates and with a heavy steel keel – on the end of the wings and the water flow on them kept the net open. A further development was floats to keep the net up. On the bottom of the nets in those days were chains or ropes with lead attached which would further help to keep the net open.

These trawl 'doors' immediately gave the fishers a big increase in their catching power. But the constant search for an ever-wider net opening to catch more fish led to the next development – 'sweeps' or wires which moved the 'doors' further away from the net.

> With modern gear you can have 120 metres (400 feet) across your trawl 'doors' and across the mouth of the net 24 metres (80 feet). That's the fishing area and with species like haddock whiting and cod there is a herding instinct and they will get herded into the path of the net. You find that a sand cloud gets disturbed by the keel of the 'doors' and that follows the wires, just on the outside of the wings, creating a barrier which fish will not swim through. That herds them into the mouth of the net.

Today the wires on each side of the trawl gear vary from 500 feet on small vessels to as much as 6,500 feet on large trawlers.

As these developments made ever-bigger nets possible it became more difficult for nets to be manhandled by the trawlermen. The introduction of the power block to Scottish fleets around 1952 became a key moment for the industry. With machinery to help haul and shoot the nets, the boats moved to new, harder fishing grounds. This put greater demands on the nets and ways had to be found to give them greater protection from seabed rocks. Rob said:

> They started to put bobbins on the bottom of the nets to protect them. You're not talking about boulder fields on the seabed, but shale with the odd stone. The bobbins were first used by the bigger vessels; these were big rubber wheels which could be up to twenty-one inches in diameter. They would trundle along the bottom and roll over any obstacle encountered.
>
> That was the traditional ground gear used in the 1960s and 1970s. It's still used to this day by some boats. But the final change was the rockhopper. That made a real difference to the performance of the nets.

Rockhoppers, saucer-shaped discs punched out of tractor tyres, are attached to a groundrope at the bottom of the net mouth and will simply jump over obstacles encountered.

One aspect of modern nets which would surprise a deckhand from the *Toiler* past would be the colour and weight. Scottish trawl nets are now made of braided polyethylene twine which comes in brightly coloured oranges and greens. Rob explained:

> It used to be nylon way, way back but the problem with nylon is that it rots and is heavy. It sinks when it gets immersed in water. Polyethylene is in effect buoyant material and that helps in terms of opening up the net.

In whitefish trawls the mesh size decreases in each section back to the cod-end at the end of the net. These are dictated by rules governing the catching of fish species. It is essential for restocking that undersized fish escape through the net. Rob said:

> In the 1970s the fishers were very conservative, sticking to the type of net which their fathers used but the Scottish fishermen, unlike the Spanish and French, are very open to new technology now and that's why they have developed twine that has got stronger and that helps to make the nets last. In some areas the Spanish are still using a net which was designed a hundred years ago.
>
> The Scottish skipper has adopted wheelhouse technology. For instance they use scanners on the nets so that they can work out its shape in the water. They are very go-ahead in terms

of net design, producing gear that is very robust and able to target the sort of fish they want to catch.

In fact the Scottish industry has become so good at net design that the fisheries researchers have stepped back from this aspect of their work. 'We were very involved in this in the 1980s,' said Rob. 'Part of our remit was to develop gear but that changed to coming up with means to allow the juvenile fish to escape the nets.'

With the full package of trawl gear, nets, wires and doors costing around £25,000 fishers know that science can help them get a net that can target as many fish species as possible. They don't want to have to stow different nets for landing different fish.

Another way science has helped the fishers is through the use of a flume tank to test scale models of nets and develop new gear. 'It allowed the generation coming into the industry in the 1980s to understand how nets worked from the scale models,' said Rob.

He believes that these days net design and twine technology is so good that there is little change needed in the net. 'It's quite notable that if someone says they have come up with a new net these days you find there is nothing radically new.'

Inevitably the conversation turned to the importance of conservation. The FRS continue to work with the industry to ensure that fish stocks remain at sustainable levels.

The image that trawlers are going out to pillage the seas is nonsense. Every fish they bring aboard they want to land. They don't want to land juvenile fish. They want to get them out of the net and that's where we work closely with the industry to achieve that aim.

All species are important to the Scottish fleet. Depending on the area fished they are looking for the likes of turbot, halibut, plaice, lemon sole, witches, megrims. You've also got haddock, whiting, saithe, cod. The fleet is very much a mixed-species fleet, it's different from our European partners. In Norway, for instance, they're not interested in haddock. Cod and saithe are their main species along with some of the flatfish species. In Denmark haddock and whiting are viewed as trash fish. They are very much targeting cod and plaice and saithe as well. In France and Spain they tend to target the likes of saithe or cod.

The Scottish fishery is traditionally a complete mixture of species and they need this to make a living. You can see that from what is being sold at Aberdeen market. And then if you look at each vessel's quota per month from its producer organisation you will see it is made up of all these different species. The Scottish fleet needs all these different species to remain viable.

That's why we have the sort of nets we use as opposed to Spain, for instance, which is targeting the fish they have always gone for. We are different from a lot of the fishing fleets around Europe.

Once again the complexities of the North Sea fishery and the difficulties of framing a Common Fisheries Policy were clear to see.

Rob Kynoch of Fisheries Research Services in Torry at Aberdeen Fish Market.

Working on a 10,000 box landing at Peterhead Fish Market in 1984. Second sales had to be held as there were so many fish.

Trawlermen hauling nets on the deck of the steam trawler *Rononia* in 1950.

Fishermen from Portknockie and Findochty mend nets under a floodlight on the *Eileen Shona* after landing a catch at Lochinver in 1977.

Repairs underway in 1972 when it was seldom that a trawl net was cast without requiring immediate attention.

Hauling the trawl before winches eased this backbreaking task.

The trawl net is pulled alongside
during fishing operations in 1972.

Preparing to take the cod-end on board the *George R. Wood* in 1972.

The floats, which help keep the mouth of the net open during trawling, come to the surface. This was the scene on the trawler *George R. Wood* in April 1972.

A catch of herring packed in wooden boxes waits on the quayside to be loaded on to fish lorries bound for the curers' yards in 1944.

HARVEST OF THE SEAS

CHAPTER TEN

HARVEST OF THE SEAS

The fish-curing firm of Allan & Dey has remained in business for well over a hundred years by being able to adapt to public tastes as ever changing as the sea itself. When it first began trading in Aberdeen in 1892 to process the fish from the burgeoning steam trawler fleet its kilns must have been busy, for by the early years of the twentieth century its finnan haddies had customers around the world.

Those famous peat-smoked haddock have now given way to high-quality fresh, frozen and smoked fish products with salmon their speciality. Managing director John Masson is bullish about a profitable company which has adapted to all the political and social changes which have buffeted the industry.

John, who started with the company in 1968, explained: 'There's a different structure these days. It's a pity we're not employing the hundreds of filleters that we once did in Aberdeen. We've gone from 200 down to 7.'

The changes in the markets for Allan & Dey products in recent decades is instructive. When John Masson, pictured, joined they were still essentially a company of smokers and exporters of whitefish. The abundant Faroese waters were still open to the Aberdeen fleet, with heavy 'shots' of the cod-like colley and cod itself arriving at the market. These were the days when the smoked fish supper was much in demand. Military contracts and a healthy Australian and Irish market also helped sustain the business.

By the 1980s and early 1990s haddock became more important after the Faroese waters closed to our trawlers. The company exported 75 per cent of its products. The USA was a multi-million pound market as convenience foods like TV dinners began to dominate the market. That market eventually became more difficult as dollar exchange rates became less favourable.

In a move which anticipated further changes in the public's eating choices Allan & Dey bought into fish farming. They now have eleven centres producing 5,000 tonnes of salmon a year. Then in the late 1990s the company bought the Edinburgh Smoked Salmon Company in Dingwall. This signalled a critical shift and instead of 75 per cent of the products being exported it was 25 per cent, with the bulk now going to United Kingdom supermarkets. Once again consumers have changed their habits and the industry had to respond.

The mode of shopping had altered with customers becoming more discerning – and more adventurous. Edinburgh Smoked Salmon, now employing 200 at the Dingwall processing plant, moved from volume cheap products to high-value fresh items.

'People are more and more quality sensitive,' said John Masson. 'Farm cod are the finest I've tasted.'

John Masson is sure that aquaculture farming is the big change of the twenty-first century for the company which started in the nineteenth century with a smoking kiln.

Improved packaging, air travel and transport companies geared to quick-turnover sorting and packaging of fresh products have kept this business able to respond to a market which can change very quickly. Dozens of different kinds of fish products now vie for the attentions of shoppers. Fish is fashionable again.

'We have gone from colley and cod to haddock for the United States,' said Mr Masson. 'We went into salmon farming. Now we're also back into fresh fish, buying it internationally and selling internationally. We're a very profitable company.'

The early days of selling fish in Aberdeen. The catches are spread out on the quayside beside the steam trawlers before being auctioned and packed into boxes for transportation.

New technology comes to Aberdeen Fish Market in 1961. Buyer Harry Craig, along with Martin Milne, phones the latest information on sales direct to their office.

Lorries are loaded up at the end of
Aberdeen market sales in 1972.

Women at work gutting
herring in Peterhead, 1938.

Teams of women hard at work gutting in an Aberdeen fish house in 1946.

Fish processing work in progress in Aberdeen on January 8, 1979.

Girls working at the Finnan kiln of Allan &
Dey in Aberdeen in 1911. The Finnan
Haddie – split, pickled and peat-smoked
haddock – was already a breakfast luxury
appreciated around the world.
(Courtesy of Allan and Dey Ltd)

It looks like a modern fish processing factory
but it is a scene below decks on an East
German factory ship, the *Junge Welt*, in 1981.
Filleting is in full swing prior to the freezing of
the fish and return to East Germany from
Scottish waters. The collapse of the
Communist countries ended this business.

The *Strathglass* steaming out of Aberdeen Harbour in the late 1940s.

GENERATIONS OF SKILLS

CHAPTER ELEVEN

GENERATIONS OF SKILLS

The trade of fishing runs through generations of families. And the skills deployed in the ancient pursuit of fish for food are surprisingly diverse. Professionalism and pride are reflected in much that is connected with the north-east's fishing industry.

One of the more pleasing crafts is the specialist boat painting which has been continued through generations of fishing families. A great admirer of this art is Douglas Paterson, chief executive of Aberdeen City Council. Like so many folk from north-east Scotland Mr Paterson comes of a fishing family. His Macduff-based kin owned and worked a succession of boats. From 1899 to 1905 they took to the waters in a two-masted decked Fifie and from 1905 to 1914 it was the Lossiemouth-designed Zulu boat *Speedwell* that they fished from. These fast boats got their unusual name because they come from the same era as the Zulu wars.

In a progression that mirrored the development of the industry the family also owned a yawl, a steam drifter and seine netters, culminating in the 55-foot seine netter/trawler *Sheigra* up to the late 1970s.

As a child in Macduff Douglas saw at first hand the pride the skippers and crews took in their boats. He also noted with fascination the skills lavished on painting the boats. This was particularly evident about forty years ago when ports from Burghead to Arbroath all boasted fleets of gleaming family-owned fishing boats.

When Douglas was growing up he had a grandfather and uncle who were skippers with their own boats and as a youth he spent a half-dozen summers working as a painter on the boats on the slipway at Macduff.

He said: 'In the early days fishermen couldn't afford to pay painters so they did their own painting.' From this grew a form of folk art with particular styles and colours becoming associated with certain ports. By tradition Buckie boats have their wheelhouses in a distinctive grained light oak yellow colour.

Wheelhouses often had panels of wood graining. This was so prevalent that it became known as 'wheelhouse wood'. A yellow stripe was commonly painted round the bulwarks of a vessel, just below the registration number. In some ports this strip was replaced with mourning blue for one fishing season if a crew member had been lost at sea.

Doubtless over the past hundred years and more, the pride which skippers and crews have in maintaining their vessels has brought a degree of competition between the boats. Names were intricately carved on boards and inlaid with gold leaf and then placed on the stern. Often an emblem was carved to represent the boat name.

Another opportunity for embellishment came with the introduction of registration letters and numbers in all fishing nations. This was so that the individual home ports of vessels – and the vessels themselves – could easily be identified. In this way 'A' now denotes an Aberdeen boat, 'PD' Peterhead, 'FR' Fraserburgh and surrounding villages, and 'BF' covers Banff, Gardenstown, Macduff and Whitehills. For example the registration number for the Zulu boat mentioned above was BF635.

The requirement to mark this identification on the boats produced signage usually picked out in white with blue shadowing. Other examples have the registration on a black panel or black with red shadowing if the boat has a light colour.

Douglas Paterson says that the purest form of this art is dying out with detailing and wood graining no longer evident. But good examples of the art can still be found in the smaller ports around the United Kingdom, and particularly in the east and north-east of Scotland and the Northern Isles.

Painting, like the naming of vessels, has changed. 'There used to be a lot of names drawn from the Bible,' said Douglas Paterson. 'But this is less the case now. There also used to be a lot related to the work ethic and flower names were common. 'I think the main current theme is amalgams of family members' names . . . sometimes with pretty awful results.'

Although he may not approve of all the names emblazoned on boats Douglas, who still has second cousins in the industry, retains a healthy respect for north-east fishermen. 'Mainly hard-working, down-to-earth and decent folk,' he said.

One veteran seaman who put the skills of his trade to use onshore is Tommy Allan of Ellon, pictured. For a number of years his net-making abilities were applied to producing and repairing goal nets for the local football teams. Former skipper Tommy, now in his nineties, also became a great favourite with schoolchildren showing them how to make knots and entertaining them with rope tricks.

The *John Morrice* passing
Aberdeen Harbour's
Round House in 1949.
She was a long-line vessel
converted to side trawler.

Douglas Paterson working on intricate signage for a boat.

Clyde-built stern trawler *Grampian Monarch* which was commissioned in 1973 for Aberdeen's George Craig Group.

The *Countesswells*, a trawler typical of the fleet in the 1960s.

The thirty-five-metre
motor vessel
Grampian Crest at sea.

Heading back to sea. A trawlerman heads for his boat at Pointlaw, Aberdeen, with a waterproof kitbag slung over his shoulder at the end of the New Year break in 1964.

Ploughing through the waves on the way to the fishing grounds.

INVESTING IN THE FUTURE

CHAPTER TWELVE

INVESTING IN THE FUTURE

It was an early spring day along the Buchan coast. The sun breaking through a light mist dispelled memories of winter and brought optimism to people's hearts. At Banff and Buchan College they were preparing for the 2007 intake of trainee trawl fishermen. The Fraserburgh-based college is the only one on mainland Britain offering such a course and things were looking up. Course tutor John Scott told me:

> When I first came here nine years ago we had two classes, that was twenty-eight young fishermen. Then it dwindled down over the years until two years ago there was only an intake of five. After that they decided to skip a couple of intakes to try to boost the numbers. Now there's much more interest in the courses and there's a good chance they will be full.

The former skipper added: 'The fishing industry is looking better. It's very encouraging. There's not so many boats and they're getting good prices for their fish. They're making good money.'

A far cry from the position just a year earlier when Fraserburgh councillor Brian Topping was appealing for help from the local authority to save the 'very important' fishing-related courses. At that time the student numbers were not high enough to make the courses viable. The council gave its full support to saving the courses.

John Scott explained that the lads on the course are employed by the North-East Fishermen's Training Association (NEFTA) which pays them for the first twelve weeks of the course before they go to sea and pass through a year and a half of assessment.

The college gives the lads training that a busy trawl crew would find hard to match. John said:

> I must have been ten years at sea before I learned to mend nets. If there was a torn net the priority was to get it back on the sea bed again catching fish. Nobody had time to teach you mending techniques. Now the trainees are getting a good start here and when they go to sea they have good hands on them.

A skipper employing a trainee from the college is looking for the basic deck skills although the course also covers learning the basics of navigation such as identifying lights, some chart work and VHF radio use. 'But apart from that,' said John 'it's splicing ropes at first and then working with wires. Beyond that we spend a lot of time on net work.'

After a fisherman has three years' sea-time behind him he can look to gain his Class Two qualification which used to be known as the Mate's Ticket. The old Skipper's Ticket is now the Class One qualification.

Future prospects for the industry, of course, depend on the availability and price of fish. Throughout my researches I heard praise for the tighter rules that had got 'blackfish' under control. These illegal landings were seen as a major cause of reducing the price of fish on the market floor and generally damaging the industry.

One of the surest signs of the fishing industry being in good heart is orders for new boats. Anyone visiting the fishing town of Macduff will be aware of two landmarks – the parish church high on a hill overlooking the harbour, and the shipyards alongside the harbour.

And all the signs at the shipyards indicated a thriving business when I visited them. In his office Bill Farquhar, a director of Macduff Shipyards Ltd, showed typical north-east reserve as he admitted to a 'bit of interest in new build'. Most enthusiasm, he said, is for prawn trawlers but whitefish vessels are also mentioned.

A trawler is no small commitment, with a basic sixty-foot vessel, without fishing licence or trawl gear, costing in the region of £1 million. For an eighty-foot boat the damage is around £3 million, depending on the specification wanted. Build time would be around a year.

In the meantime the yards are kept healthily busy with year-round repair work on fishing boats on top of orders for boats from sixty to ninety-five feet.

The company is by no means tied entirely to the fishing industry. When I visited, three steel ships were being built – a research vessel for Aberdeen, a multi-purpose vessel for Perth Harbour which was shortly going to sea trials, and a buoy tender destined for Wales.

Macduff Shipyards has a long and respected history stretching back sixty-five years. The firm built up a reputation for wooden fishing boats. Indeed it can boast of having been the last yard in the UK to build wooden fishing boats over 56 feet. There are no wooden boats on the stocks at present but Bill Farquhar does not rule out the possibility of wooden boats being built in the future.

These days the four directors own the company. They all work in the yard and have 130 years of experience in the business between them. The company has gradually built up over the years and tries to do as much in-house as possible.

In the time the company has been in operation the design of vessels has changed considerably. Bill said: 'Every builder adapts to changes dictated by the buyers. These days there's more emphasis on the quality of fish landed.'

Another vital factor is the high cost of fuel. When prices are steadily rising and boats can easily use 600 to 1,000 gallons a week, anything to save on that expense is welcome. So bigger, more economical, propellers are favoured just now. Bill said that crew comfort and increased mechanisation are also big considerations as the north-east trawler continues to evolve.

Macduff Shipyards Ltd, with its 130 employees, busy yards and a repair facility in Fraserburgh, is another part of the complex jigsaw of innovation and hard work which ensures a future for the north-east fishing industry.

John Scott, lecturer at Banff and Buchan College.

The historic steam ship *Explorer* at the breakers yard Inverkeithing in 1985. The Aberdeen-built vessel is one of the last of the seagoing steam trawlers. After a long campaign the trawler is now being restored at Leith to preserve part of our maritime history.

Director Bill Farquhar at the Macduff shipbuilders yard.

The Aberdeen steam trawler *Kinord*. Note the small bridge and open decks of that era.

The share-owned *Red Crusader*, sister ship of the Aberdeen trawler *Blue Crusader* which was lost with all thirteen crew on a trip to the Faroe Islands in 1965.

The motor trawler *Parkroyd* that was purchased from Hull and added to the Aberdeen fleet.

DEDICATIONS

Malcolm Adamson

Robert William Allen

Stewart Anderson

Wilma Anderson

William Arthur

Russell Balls (2nd Fish)

Bobby Barnie (Deck)

Alan Barron

Johnny Baxter

Sandy Beaton

Stanley Bennington

James Black

Jim Bowie

Billy Brechin

James Brown

William J Bruce

George C Buchan

George West Buchan

John W Buchan

Thomas Reid Buchan

Allan Cardno

Stuart F Chalmers

Chelino

John Alexander Clark

Lawrence Clark

Margaret Souter Clark

William Clarke

Alfred John Clifton

Alfred Charles Clifton

George Ross Connell

Lena Cooper

Jim Couper

William D Cowe Senior

Alexander Cowie

James Cowie

John Cowie

Raymond Stephen Crombie

Frankie Davidson (Deck)

Les Davidson

Leslie Davidson

Charlie Dawson

Norman (Norrie) Deans

John Donaldson

Billy Duguid

Albert Duncan

Ronnie Duncan

Walter Duncan

James Dustan

Ian Duthie

James Duthie

Michael Elder

William Elder

David Main Ellen

Michael Ewen

Mr & Mrs D Falconer

James G G Farquhar

William Farquhar

Douglas Farquharson

George Fleming

Alexander Forbes

Malcolm G Forbes

Elizabeth I Forbes

Duncan Ford

Stewart Ford

George Fowlie

Alistair Fraser

Daisy and Jim Fraser

Charles Fraser (Stocker)

Cecil Garson

William Gault

Bobby Gibb (Chf Eng)

Alexander Gordon

Stanley Gordon

Ramsay Grant

Duncan (Kenzie) Gray

John Gray

Charles Grimmer Snr

James R Grimmer Snr

Frank Hale

Crawford Kenzie Henderson

Netta Henderson

William Oliver Henry

Aiden Hodgins

Billy Holland

Raymond Holland

William Holland

T H Hutchison

James Alexander Imlach

Mike Irvine

David Jack

Isabella Jaffray

Joseph Jappy

John

Ted Jones

Alex Keay

Margaret Keith

Colin Kelday

Gerald Kelday

Norman Kelday

George Kennedy

Ronald Lawrence

David Lawson

Michael Leaburn

Peter Leask

Ronald Leitch

George Lemmon (Budgie) Eng

Alexander Leslie

Mr Raymond Leslie

Charles Low (Spud) Deck

George MacDonald

Roy MacGregor

Angus M MacIntosh

Donald MacKay

Simon MacLeod

Kenneth A MacLennan

David B MacMillan

William (Bill) McAllan

James McCusker

Alistair McGee

Frank McGeough

David McKenzie

Mike McLean

David McLennan

William David McLennan

Danny McPherson

Grace McPherson

James McPherson

Scott McPherson

William McPherson

Leslie McRobbie (Deck)

Jim McRonald

Norman McSwayde

Billy Magee

James Main

Alexander Mair

Skipper Bill Mair (Cullen)

John Mair

Alan N Maison

Elsie Manson

James Manson

Henry Marshall

Arthur Massie

James (Sonny) G Matheson

John Menhinick

James Alexander Miller

Arthur Milne

William W Milne

Roy Mitchell

William Mitchell

Malcolm MacLean Morrison

Murray

David and Lois Murray

George Murray

James Murray

Mike Murray

Bruce Neptune

James Watson Nicol

Jim Nicolson

Jim Niddrie

George Noble

Florence Norquay

Norman Norquay

William Alexander Ord

Michael O'Sullivan

Iain-Neil Paterson

Gordon R Penny

Duncan Pockett

John Prosser

Frankie Rae (Teapot) Deck

Aimee Reid

Gerald Rennie

John Robert (Jack) Ribee

John Richmond

James Bertrum Riley

Marc Ritchie

Anne and Andy Robertson

Billy Robertson

Jim Robertson

Stanley Robertson

Struan J T Robertson

Roddie

Bob & Andy Ross

Robert Isaac Burwood Ross

Hugh MacLean Russell

Danny Scott

Michael Scott

Thomas Scott (Sen)

Thomas Scott (Jun)

Shep

Alexander Shirran

Billy Shirran (D/H)

Jim Shirron

Bill Simmonds

Abby Slater (Capt.)

Alistair Slater

Jozie-Anne Smart

Sean Smart

Krista Lee Smart

Alexander Smith

Bill Smith

Bryn Smith

Edward Smith

George Smith

George C Smith

Ivor Smith

Joseph Smith

Larry Smith

Ally Souter

Hilary Souter

John Spink

Frederick Spratt

Robert Hamish Stanger

Andy Stephen (Teapot) Deck

Billy Stephen (Teapot) Cook

George Stephen (Teapot) Skip

George Stephen (Teapot) Eng

George Stephen (Teapot) Deck

John Stephen

Ian Stewart

May Stewart

Kevin Stirton

Edmund Walter Strachan

Michael Stroud

Ian Summers

Tom Sutherland

William Sutherland

Marelle & Gavin Tarburn

Dan Taylor

William Taylor

Andrew James Thomson

George Thomson

Jim Thomson

George Tytler

William Uren

Andrew Walker

Mr William M S Walker

Frank Watson

Stan Watt

Gordon Watters

Isabel Watts

Colin Watts

Brian and Hazel Wilkins

Margaret Wilkinson

Robert Williamson

Stephen Wilson

Alistair Beattie Wood

David Mitchell Wood

Gerald Woodcock

Sheila Woodcock

Stephen Wright

BIBLIOGRAPHY

Anyone writing about the fishing industry will very soon discover they are in well-charted waters. Here are some of the sources I found invaluable in my researches:

Anson, Peter, *Fishing Boats and Fisher Folk* (JM Dent and Sons Ltd, 1930)

Anson, Peter, *Scots Fisherfolk* (Publisher, 1932 and Saltire Society publications 1950)

Baxter, Andrew, *Bygone Days of Footdee* (transcript)

Buchan, A. R., The Port of Peterhead, 1977

Creswell, Jeremy, *Time and Tide, The Story of the Craig Group* (privately published)

Fraser, W. Hamish and Clive H. Lee (eds), *Aberdeen 1800–2000; A New History* (Tuckwell Press, 2000)

Galbraith, R. D., Rice, A, Strange, E. S., *An Introduction to Commercial Fishing Gear and methods used in Scotland* (Scottish Fisheries Information Pamphlet, 2004)

Kilgour, Ethel, *A Time of Our Lives* (City of Aberdeen, 1992)

Kurlansky, Mark, *Cod* (Vintage, 1998)

Morgan, Diane, *Footdee, The Villages of Aberdeen,* (Denburn Books, 1993)

Pyper, William, *History of a Great Industry* (Privately, 1903)

The Third Statistical Account of Scotland, 1960

Smith, Robert, *One Foot in the Sea,* (John Donald, 1991)

Trewren, Norman, *The Lifeline – History of Aberdeen Lifeboat Station 1925–85* (Privately published, 1985)

FINAL TRAWL

Now it's three long years since we made her pay
       Sing haul away my laddie oh
And the owners say that she's had her day
       And sing haul away my laddie oh

So heave away for the final trawl
it's an easy pull for the catch is small.

Then stow your gear lads and batten down
and we'll say farewell to the fishing grounds.

We'll join the *Venture* and the *Morning Star*
riding high and empty beyond the bar.

For I'd rather beach her on the Skerry Rock
than to see her torched in the breaker's dock.

And when I die you can stow me down
in her rusty hold where the breakers pound.

Then I'll make the haven of Fiddler's Green
where the rum is good and the bunks are clean.

For I've fished a lifetime boy and man
and the final trawl barely nets a cran.

Archie Fisher
Copyright © Kettle Music

NO MORE TIE-UPS

Fishermen don't put your boats out to sea
there's a storm on the rise.
The tide's on the turn and the wind's come away
there's turmoil ahead in the sky.
It could be a day or a week or an age
as we wait for the gale to come round.
There's mouths to be fed
and there's bills to be paid
before we return to the grounds

Chorus:
Roll the ocean, roll the sea
Roll the ocean, roll the sea

Living's not easy with quotas cut down
and prices so low on the quay.
To sell up and move on could be the best way
if we knew more than life on the sea
As the trawlers evolve with their satcom and sonar
it's hard toil with hauler and creel.
And the smaller boats forced into treacherous waters
the inner lochs long ago gleened.

Chorus
The ocean's a safe place for each man and all
if treated with care and respect.
But with tie-ups and curfews enforced on more sectors
you've got to chance fate on the deck.
Captain and crew are all one and the same
when it comes down to sharing a pay.
For the harder your toil and the longer you steam
the more chance of taking a wage.

Wolfstone
Copyright © Struan W. Eaglesham MCPS/PRS